IN THIS ISSUE

LA+ PLEASURE
EDITORIAL

Inside the original garden of paradise there was no pain, *ipso facto* no pleasure. As Lisa Shapiro explains in her introductory essay, Adam's bliss was based in oblivion. But pleasure is something else: awareness of one's surroundings and of pleasure's counterparts – pain, toil and, ultimately, mortality.

If you Google 'paradise' you find images of white beaches, clear skies, and azure waters. There are no animals, few plants, and no people – apart from the proverbial Eve, scantily clad and in conspicuously good health. With this image in mind, tourists have now trampled the world's coastlines causing the development of tourist-oriented coastal urban centers. As C. Michael Hall and his colleagues argue, for these tourist paradises to survive "the changing fashions of tourist taste," they must integrate tourism with sustainable urban planning. But why travel at all when, as we see in the case of Discovery Bay in Hong Kong, new developments appropriate the style of the resort and deliver it to your doorstep?

Urbanism and paradise find their best partnership in the works of 19th-century landscape architecture, where arcadia is rendered innocent and democratic. The apotheosis of this is Central Park, conceived to pull the masses back from the debauchery that Coney Island and Atlantic City took to such extraordinary heights. Randall Mason and Josephine Kane recall these now dilapidated coastal amusements on both sides of the Atlantic. Against the backdrop of Central Park we can also now read the designs for New York City's most recent parks, reviewed in this issue by Ellen Neises. In these projects we see landscape architects breaking free of what Phoebe Lickwar and Thomas Oles describe as landscape architecture's "lugubrious sermons" and its "quest to save."

In tales of other cities, philosopher Mark Kingwell maps a psycho-geography of Toronto in a paean to the Situationists; historian Ray Laurence encourages a reading of Rome through an Epicurean rather than Stoic lens, charting its development as an urban pleasurescape from Julius Ceasar to Augustus; and Richard Campanella describes how the geography of pleasure continues to evolve in New Orleans. Following this line of inquiry, Stefan Al takes us to that infamous capital of pleasure, Las Vegas, describing how its larrikin casino developers have successfully changed their methods of mass seduction over time, and Jerry Van Eyck discusses how !melk's recent scheme has at last brought a landscape architectural sense of place to the Las Vegas Strip.

Delving deeper into the dark side of pleasure, Magdalena Sabat charts the ways in which the sex industry operates both visibly and invisibly in our cities, affected as it is by spatial regulation, and we interview Czech landscape architect Vladimir Sitta, who has devoted his entire career to what could surely be described as the *masochism of the garden*. We find perhaps the deepest and darkest pleasures on the other side of the world in Australia's Museum of Old and New Art – a subterranean labyrinth that architect Mark Raggatt describes as teetering on the edge of "pleasure and pain, between sex and death." And finally, this dichotomy of pleasure and pain is explored through an extraordinary collaboration between neuroscientist Morten Kringelbach and artist Annie Cattrell, who together create artworks that shed new light on the architecture of the brain's pleasure network.

In this pious age of ecological crisis, this issue of *LA+* reminds readers of landscape architecture's complicated relationship to the theme of pleasure and—as is the mission of the journal—draws productive links between landscape architecture and other disciplines.

Tatum L. Hands
Editor in Chief

WHAT IS

LISA SHAPIRO

Lisa Shapiro is Professor of Philosophy at Simon Fraser University, Canada. She is editor of the *Oxford Philosophical Concepts* volume on pleasure (in press) and is interested in how the passions figure in 17th- and 18th-century accounts of human nature and human understanding. Shapiro is co-editor of *Emotion and Cognitive Life in Medieval and Early Modern Philosophy* (2012), and editor and translator of *The Correspondence of Princess Elisabeth of Bohemia and Rene Descartes* (2007).

✛ PHILOSOPHY, AESTHETICS

Pleasure feels good. Isn't that all we need to know in answer to the question: What is pleasure? We might want to add something about what that good feeling does for us. In most cases, pleasure provides that push, a motivation to action. We pursue pleasure, and, equally, we avoid what will prevent us from feeling good. This way of thinking about pleasure is all around us, from the design of the subway car to the incentive structures of our tax systems. If we want people to take public transit, we might upholster the seating in colorful, artistic textiles, making the experience more pleasant. Alternatively, we might provide a tax deduction for buying monthly transit passes, hoping that the pleasure of keeping more money in their pocket will give people the incentive to change the way they commute. Of course, sometimes pleasure makes us stop short—as when we stand before the saturated colors in a Titian painting—and embrace stillness. But even this sort of pleasure seems to fit the model. We take pleasure in contemplating what is before us, we might think, and so are moved to change course and stop to continue that contemplation.

Despite this common-sensical way of thinking of pleasure, even the handful of examples just considered brings out some of its problems. Is the pleasure we might take in a daily experience of artistic textiles the same sort of thing as the pleasure we take in holding on to our money, or contemplating a piece of art? Perhaps we might say that there is only one kind of pleasure, but the pleasures each of us feels can differ in degree or intensity. So some people find more pleasure in saving money while others find more pleasure in interesting textiles. Good public policy might want to get as many people riding transit as possible and so opt to provide incentives to both sorts of people. The problems emerge when we start to consider being able to choose only one incentive structure. How would we choose? One way would be to do some market research to determine which source of pleasure would influence more people; are more people likely to ride transit if the experience was more art-filled or if doing so involved a tax break? This sort of approach assumes that there is nothing more to say than that people feel the pleasures they do, the market researchers are analyzing the demographic profile. While in some cases there is simply a fact about what a person finds pleasing (a person might find vanilla ice cream more pleasing than strawberry, for instance), many of our pleasures invite questions. Once we start analyzing the reasons for our pleasures, we are quickly led to questions about whether we *ought* to feel those pleasures, about whether our reasons are good ones. These questions take pleasure to have a normative dimension. And we might think that the answers to the normative questions about pleasure are needed to decide whether to reupholster the transit seating or offer a tax deduction. Market research is not going to help settle what pleasures *ought* to guide our policies.

Opposite: *The Fall of Man* by Titian (1570).

PLEASURE?

Considering the question of what pleasures we *ought* to feel leads quite quickly into thinking that perhaps pleasure is not *one* thing, and that rather there are many kinds of pleasures. The pleasure taken in artistic textiles might just be a different kind of pleasure than that in saving money, and we might want to promote one over the other. Indeed, Plato's later dialogue *Philebus*, which is focused on pleasure, effectively suggests that pleasure is not one thing, but rather there are different kinds of pleasures, from the pleasure that contributes to survival, to the pleasure that guides our choices, to the true pleasure found in pure mathematics. While this view is only left implicit in *Philebus*, one can read Aristotle as developing this point. On Aristotle's view, pleasure is an aspect of activities we undertake, namely, what an activity gains when there is a fit between the capacity being activated, say, hearing, and what it is activated in relation to, say, music: we take pleasure in hearing a fine piece of music because there is a good fit between our capacity for hearing and that music. Our pleasures, then, will be as varied as are our capacities. Another central figure from ancient philosophy, Epicurus, however, rejects the idea that there are many kinds of pleasure, and advances the view that the many pleasures we feel differ only in degree or intensity and so can always be ranked relative to one another.

Let me return to the normative dimension of pleasure intrinsic to the question, "What *ought* we to take pleasure in?" Part of the reason we end up asking this question is because pleasure can and does mislead us. I take a bite of a decadent chocolate cake, savoring the flavor, the texture, the wave of warmth the cocoa brings, and so I take another bite aiming to sustain the feeling of pleasure, and then another, and then I've overindulged. You become engrossed in a novel, turning page after page, enjoying the world unfolding in the book as time passes without notice, but then you find you've neglected everything else – you needed to mark papers, make dinner, walk the dog. In these sorts of cases we want to say that pleasure led us astray, but how? Did the pleasure capture us, so that we could do or think of nothing else? This doesn't seem quite right: in eating the cake, I was focused on the texture and the taste as much as the pleasure I felt. In reading the novel, you were thinking of the characters and the narrative, as well as taking pleasure in the story. We feel pleasure along with other experiences we might be having. But still, there is something about pleasure that can gain control of us, and so explain our being misguided.

So what is it about pleasure that explains my eating more chocolate cake or your being engrossed in your novel? Those who think that pleasure is a simple, analyzable feeling claim that in these sorts of cases the pleasure has become so intense, so strong, that it stifles all other signals. I've already suggested that there are problems with this line of thinking. Another option is to think that the feeling of pleasure is not unanalyzable, but rather is about something, and in particular is about, or represents, our own good. In feeling pleasure in eating the chocolate cake, we represent the cake as good; in feeling pleasure in reading the novel,

we represent that activity as good. So, we might think of pleasure as similar to other sensory experiences. Just as our sense of vision represents shapes and colors, and our sense of hearing represents sounds, so does our ability to sense pleasure represent particular things as good for us. When we eat too much cake or become over-engrossed in a novel, we are misrepresenting what is good for us in some way, in these cases by exaggerating the degree to which something is good. But we might also imagine cases in which we feel pleasure in something that is just bad for us: if natural gas were imbued with the smell of roses instead of the smell of sulfur, we could imagine feeling pleasure even while inhaling the dangerous substance.

Thinking of pleasure as representing our good can help clarify the normative dimension of pleasure; for the notion of our good itself contains a normative standard. We can judge someone to have fallen short if they fail to take pleasure in something that is good for them, just as we can judge that they have felt a degree of pleasure disproportionate to the good of, say, the chocolate cake or a novel. Perhaps we might want to say that the person who takes more pleasure in a modest tax rebate than in attractive transit seating has a skewed sense of their own good. Note, though, that the good that pleasure represents on this view is not some timeless and true Good, but rather *our* good, a good that is indexed to human beings, and potentially even indexed to individual human beings. Things need not be good for all human beings in the same way, and the same thing can be good for a single individual in different ways at different points in her life. This variation in the way things are good for each of us will come along with variations in experiences of pleasure. More will need to be said about this normative dimension of pleasure, of the proper limits of our ability to judge others' experiences of pleasure. But if pleasure really is akin to sense perception we should be optimistic about the prospect of doing this. After all, people see shapes and color and hear sounds differently from one another, and we are still able to tolerate a range of appropriate perceptions while still maintaining that individuals can mis-see or mis-hear.

There might, however, be another challenge in thinking of pleasure as akin to sensation. We find some colors more pleasant than others; as anyone who has spent some time with paint chips can attest, there is a difference in the 'feel' of a warm shade of a white and a stark, clinical white. What is happening in these sorts of cases? Are we having two sensations—one of color, and another of pleasure—or just one sensation? It certainly seems as if the pleasure is not a separate sensation but is rather, in some sense, a part of our sensation of color. We can't look at certain colors without feeling a pleasure, nor can we feel the pleasure detached from the color. Perhaps, then, pleasure is not so much a sensation as a *manner* of perceiving. My perception of the white is a pleasant one; that is, I am seeing the white pleasantly. And similarly, I am hearing a piece of music pleasantly, and so on.

Here's what seems right about this way of thinking about pleasure: pleasure infuses our experiences, and isn't separable from them. And the intensity of pleasure informs what we perceive. If we find a piece of music particularly pleasurable, we will hear things in it, and in performances of it, that we would not if it were a less-pleasant listening experience. Nonetheless, it is hard to explain just what this pleasant manner of perceiving amounts to.

Perhaps a bit surprisingly, a discussion by 17th-century philosopher Nicolas Malebranche of the Fall of Man in the Garden of Eden might be able to help with this question.[1] We are all familiar with a story in which Adam succumbs to the temptation of pleasure, and eats fruit from the Tree of Knowledge of Good and Evil. Eve is presented as a kind of seductress, enticing Adam to indulge in this pleasure, as has been strictly forbidden by God. This is not Malebranche's story; indeed, Eve barely makes an appearance. Malebranche tells the story thus: in the Garden of Eden, Adam felt pleasure all the time, to immediately inform him about what was good for him. With this information coming in directly, he could survive without having to think, and his attention could be directed fully towards God. However, instead of continuing to feel pleasure this way, Adam turned away from contemplating God to behold the apple itself and to take delight, or feel pleasure, in doing so. That is, rather than simply sensing the apple as a vehicle of nourishment, Adam's pleasure transformed as he began to focus on the apple, as an object, with properties to be discovered. For Malebranche, original sin is just noticing things around us in such a way that we are moved to find out more about them, to pursue knowledge. Noticing things in this way involves a particular sort of pleasure, but this sort of pleasure is quite special. It is not simply one manner of perceiving things among many. It is the manner of perceiving things as things. Pleasure is awareness of the world around us.

1 See Nicolas Malabranche, *The Search After Truth*, ed. and transl. by Thomas Lennon & Paul Olscamp [Cambridge: Cambridge University Press, 1997], Book I, Ch. 5.

MORTEN KRINGELBACH + ANNIE CATTRELL

ANARCHIT

PLEASURE

ECTURE OF
AND PAIN

COMBINING ART AND SCIENCE TO MAKE SENSE OF THE BRAIN

Morten L. Kringelbach is a Professor and Senior Research Fellow in the Department of Psychiatry at the University of Oxford, UK, and Professor of Neuroscience at the Centre for Functionally Integrative Neuroscience at the University of Aarhus, Denmark. His prizewinning research on the brain mechanisms of pleasure uses a range of behavioral, neuroimaging, neurosurgical, and computational methods. He is a Fellow of the Association for Psychological Science and a member of the advisory board of *Scientific American*. He has published 13 books and over 250 papers and articles.

Annie Cattrell is a visual artist who has exhibited internationally in public museums and galleries. She has undertaken major commissions including for the Biochemistry Department at Oxford University. Cattrell was the first Leverhulme Artist in Residence at the Royal Institution of Great Britain. She is Reader in Fine Art, and Research Group Leader in Fine Art and Photography, at DeMontfort University, UK, and a Fellow of the Royal British Society of Sculptors. See www.pleasurecentre.org.

✚ NEUROSCIENCE, PSYCHOLOGY, SCULPTURE, 3D-PRINTING, SIMULATION

Pleasure and pain are at the heart of subjective experience and the subject of much great art. Fundamentally, they are linked to the very fabric of the human brain through the architecture of the mind. Brain imaging has begun to map, in time and space, the intricate neural connectivity and choreography that bring about the complexity of emotion and higher brain function. Novel brain scanning technology coupled with whole-brain computational modeling have started to provide unique windows to the underlying cycles of brain activity linked to states of wanting, liking, and learning. In a series of works, we have explored the possibilities for three-dimensional visualization of the underlying brain architecture. Here, we present some of the fundamental new scientific results and how artistic interpretation helped us to shed new light on fundamental questions regarding the pleasure network.

Pleasure Networks

The pursuit of pleasure is universal throughout the animal kingdom. This suggests that pleasure is a fundamental principle of brain function, facilitating the survival of species and individuals.[1] Perhaps most importantly, pleasure helps us make decisions, optimizing the allocation of brain resources for efficient behavior. Pleasure can be thought of as evolution's boldest trick for sustaining and nourishing interest in the things most important to survival. Yet, pleasure has long been regarded as too subjective to be studied scientifically.

This has changed over the last 15 years, where much progress has been made in mapping the functional neuroanatomy and neurochemistry of pleasure in humans and other mammals.[2] Central to this research program has been the rise of new brain scanning techniques as well as the realization that pleasure reactions can be measured in other animals, and even in babies.

The research has demonstrated the existence of at least three major sub-components: wanting, liking, and learning, which are subserved by partly dissociable brain networks that wax and wane in influence over brain resource allocation throughout the so-called pleasure cycle. Within these networks, some regions can causally change pleasure reactions and the motivation for reward, while other regions simply code the subjective experience. In addition, research in rodents has also demonstrated the presence of so-called hedonic hotspots and coldspots, which can change pleasure reactions. These hedonic hotspots and coldspots are linked together in what could perhaps be described as an architecture of pleasure, where some of the hotspots are more important than others.

Understanding the interactions between regions in normal pleasure networks can give insight into what happens in disease. The lack of pleasure, *anhedonia*, is a major component in mental illnesses such as depression and anxiety. Treatments of mood disorders will benefit if brain mechanisms of pleasure can be understood. But more than that, a better understanding of pleasure and reward is essential to understanding fundamental biological principles of how the brain works.

Previous Page: *From Within*, by Annie Cattrell
Opposite: *Pleasure/Pain*, by Annie Cattrell and Morten Kringelbach

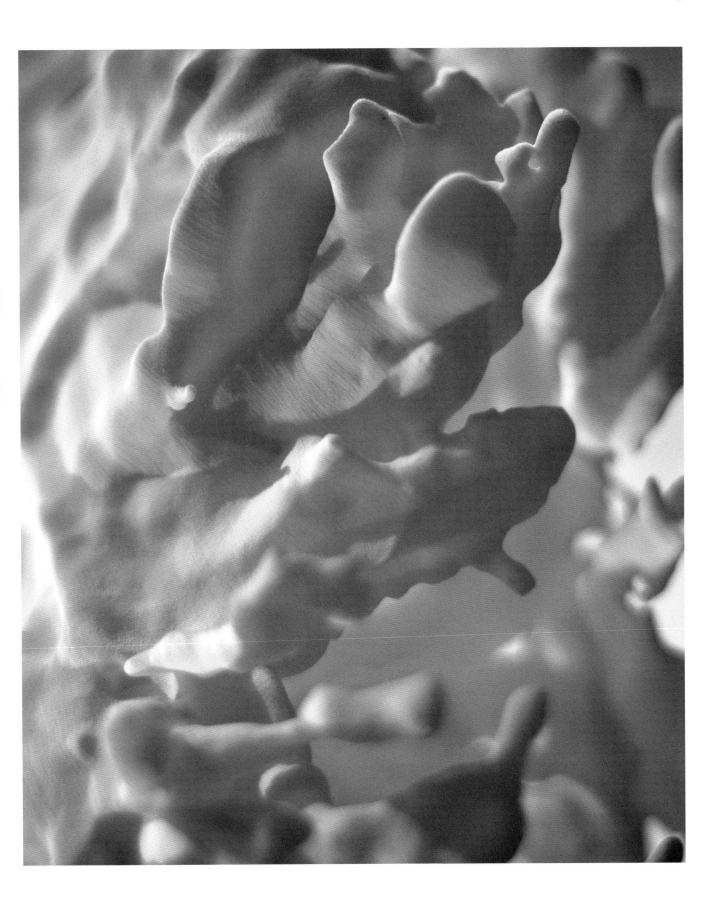

Exploring the Architecture of the Mind

Subjective experience relies on sensory impressions, but the associated pleasure is never merely a sensation; rather it is an additional hedonic gloss generated by the brain. This was also the starting point of our collaboration, and specifically how information from different senses is linked to different parts of the brain. We used functional neuroimaging of the living brain to track the spatial patterns and volumes of brain information arising from seeing, hearing, touching, smelling, and tasting. In this way we were able to map a kind of portrait of what it is like to experience the world from within. We used rapid prototyped (three-dimensional) printing to create the shape of each sensory activity map in amber-colored resin and cast (or embedded) them into five transparent resin cubes to create the artwork *Sense*.

But our collaboration was not merely an artistic mapping of territory but also a scientific exploration of what subjective experience might mean. Through the collaboration, an important organizational principle of brain function was crystallized: sensory identity is computed before and independently of subsequent hedonic processing. In other words, activity in the primary cortical regions for each of the senses remains stable and is not modulated by subsequent hedonic processing. If it were not so, we would be unable to identify chocolate once we had been sated on chocolate and temporarily do not want any.

Equally profoundly, mapping the functional activity associated with the five classical senses in three dimensions had the effect of alerting us to the importance of the large unknown regions on our functional brain maps. This is where the sensory information past and present is evaluated and where choices and decisions can be made about future actions. As the old mapmakers would have it about these great regions of unknown: "Here be dragons!" Except, of course, that these regions are starting to be mapped now. In the years that followed *Sense*, we have used a range of neuroimaging and neurosurgical techniques to map hedonic processing. Not only do we now have a better understanding of the nature of the computations performed in hedonic processing, we are also starting to be able to harness this power to change the hedonic experience.

Using deep brain stimulation of the periaqueductal grey in the brainstem, we are able to change the subjective experience of chronic pain patients. At low frequencies (<50Hz) we can induce pain relief while higher frequencies (>90Hz) have the opposite effect, inducing even worse pain. Hedonic processing such as pain and pleasure must therefore be linked in a deep way in the organization of the brain, and a fuller understanding might tell us something deep about the nature of subjective experience.

A.

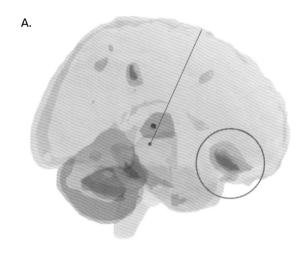

B.

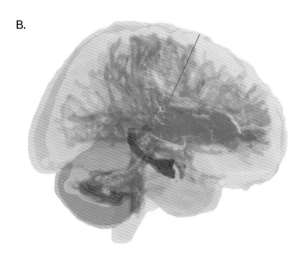

Above: Pleasure and pain in the brain: (A) shows the areas of brain activity when a deep brain stimulator is turned on to alleviate severe phantom limb pain. The circled area is the orbitofrontal cortex, which is a central part of the pleasure network in humans. (B) is a three-dimensionally reconstructed DTI image showing the areas of the brain connected to the region stimulated.

Opposite: *Sense*, by Annie Cattrell and Morten Kringelbach

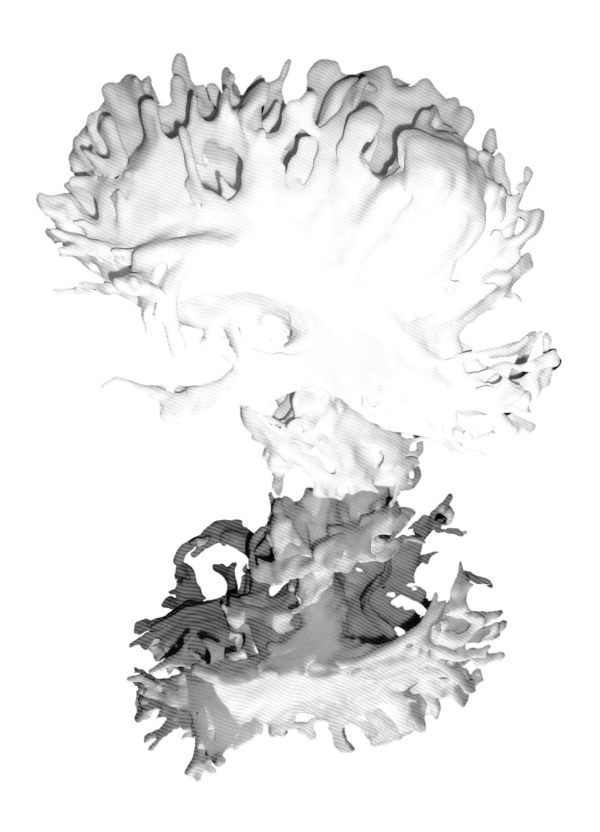

In *Pleasure/Pain* we took the data generated by a neuroimaging technique called diffusion tensor imaging (DTI) to map the structural connections of this small brain region in the brainstem. The sculpture is thus a three-dimensional reconstruction of the *structural* connections of this pivotal brain region. DTI is not a functional measure, like those used in *Sense*, but is rather an image of the structural connections that can be used by this brain region. Functional activity is played out on this structural backbone, but which of these patterns will become active depends on the spatiotemporal choreography of activity.

We are starting to map and understand the nature of the oscillations in this choreography over time. In a healthy brain, neurons in the networks communicate back and forth in an intricate call and response with groups of neurons in other brain regions. All these brain areas play a role in hedonic processing, and must work together to produce hedonic experience. These oscillations of neural activity bounce back and forth, moving at different frequencies, some serving to initiate movement, others to moderate it, but what is key is that the sender and recipient neurons–like two children rhythmically swinging a jump rope for a third to hop over–must be in sync. The dynamics of these states can be described using mathematical concepts of criticality. The brain operates best when the brain network is critical; that is, at the border of a dynamical bifurcation point, so that, at that operating point, the system defines a meaningful dynamic repertoire that is inherent to the neuroanatomical connectivity.[3]

To create the artwork *Pleasure/Pain*, we used a rapid prototyping method called selective laser sintering, which is perhaps best described as a kind of sculptural photocopying, where cross-sectional layers are fused to create a solid model. The shape is in some ways surprisingly similar to other biological shapes, such as that of a dried globe amaranth (*Gomphrena globosa*) posthumously unfolding in a glass teapot. The sculpture and image is meant to be similarly open, showing the possibilities inherent in a tea flower unfolding over time in hot water – and in the pleasures afforded by this simple, yet complex structural network.

Writing in *Nature*, the art historian Martin Kemp suggested that *Pleasure/Pain*, arising from the kind of dialogue and investigations described here, shows that "art can be as rationally founded as Renaissance theorists insisted, and that science can be as suggestively open as the act of looking itself."[4] Only time will tell, but Art and Science have much in common, perhaps not dissimilar to the pain and pleasure that goes into creating them.[5]

1 M.L. Kringelbach & K.C. Berridge, *Pleasures of the Brain* (New York: Oxford University Press, 2010).

2 M.L. Kringelbach & K.C. Berridge, "A Joyful Mind," *Scientific American* 307, no. 2 (2012): 40–45.

3 G. Deco & M.L. Kringelbach, "Great Expectations: Using Whole-Brain Computational Connectomics for Understanding Neuropsychiatric Disorders," *Neuron* 84 (2014): 892–905.

4 M. Kemp, "A Flowering of Pleasure and Pain," *Nature* 465 (2010): 295.

5 M.L. Kringelbach & H. Phillips, *Emotion: Pleasure and Pain in the Brain* (Oxford: Oxford University Press, 2014).

Opposite: *Pleasure/Pain* by Annie Cattrell and Morten Kringelbach

RAY LAURENCE

BREAD AND

URBANISM AND PLEASURE IN ANCIENT ROME

CIRCUSES

Ray Laurence is Professor of Roman History and Archaeology at the University of Kent. Over the last decade he has developed a thesis that pleasure was a driving cultural force in Roman society and the development of public space, as articulated in *Roman Passions: A History of Pleasure in Imperial Rome* (2009). Laurence's other works include *Roman Pompeii: Space and Society* (1994), *The Roads of Roman Italy: Mobility and Cultural Change* (1999), *Rome, Ostia, Pompeii: Movement and Space* (2011), and *The City in the Roman West* (2011).

✚ HISTORY, ARCHAEOLOGY

Previous Page: Church at the Baths of Diocletian

"B read and circuses," it was said, were the only interests of the Roman people; they were, after all, provided with free grain and had a circus that could seat 250,000 spectators. This reductive view expressed by the elite writer Tacitus remains an iconic value attached to imperial Rome, with its citizens unable to vote from 14 CE. However, if reductive, it expresses a concept of urbanism that placed an emphasis on the need to feed and entertain the one million people who inhabited Europe's first metropolis. This was not an action of utility, but one to remove the pain of hunger and provide the pleasure of entertainment to the greatest number of people. This conception of the provision of free food and entertainment can be understood in a number of ways: as an action rooted in the philosophy of Epicurus that pain was to be avoided, that providing enjoyment for others was a thing of merit, and that pleasure as a phenomenon did not need a justification through argument.[1]

This paper sets out to provide a means of understanding the city of Rome through an Epicurean lens, establishing pleasure as a use-value to explain the development of Rome in the late 1st century BCE and early 1st century CE. Contrarily, most modern writing on the city of Rome takes a fundamentally Stoic position: that pleasure can be gained only from (hard) work and that any activity needs to have a function. The presentation of the Epicurean position on urbanism allows us to appreciate that writing on the city in antiquity was part of a philosophical debate, and that pleasure in the Epicurean sense may indeed underlie ancient Rome's urban policies.

Epicurus and the City

The reasoning behind the development of ancient Rome as a landscape of pleasure can be identified in elite culture's relationship with Hellenistic philosophy. In the 1st century BCE and 1st century CE, we can find a variety of philosophies that had been acquired from the Hellenistic world that were seen as directly affecting the actions of members of the elite. With a varied menu of thinking, from Plato to Stoicism and on to Epicureanism, there were a variety of options that shaped Roman thinking. The provision of bread and water to the city removed for its inhabitants the distress of hunger and thirst, and created for the population the possibility of pleasure. Pleasure was not something confined to the elite: Cicero noted that the humblest people derived pleasure from knowledge of history with no hope of utilizing that knowledge for a career in public life.[2] The Epicurean might teach that pleasure is good just as snow is cold or honey is sweet – there was no necessity for pleasure to be of utility: it was of itself good, because it was pleasure.[3]

The Stoic City from Cicero to Lewis Mumford

The Epicurean position on pleasure contrasts with the Stoic position, by which virtue might be achieved through actions, and in which pleasure was equated with vice as the opposite of virtue. Historians of ancient Rome have tended to take a rather Stoic view of Roman urbanism as a description of what happened, rather than understanding these statements as a philosophical debate between different schools of thought. Thus, Lewis Mumford saw bread and circuses through a Stoic lens—coinciding with modern values associated with hard work being preferable to idleness—in which Rome is explained as a parasitical city, rather than as an Epicurean city of pleasure.[4] The problem, though, goes further and can be found in my own work, as well as that of other Roman historians; we too easily see passages that are fundamentally Stoic argumentation, such as this by Seneca, as a means to understand the city:

> Virtue is something lofty, elevated and regal, invincible and indefatigable; Pleasure is something lowly and servile, feeble and perishable, which has its base and residence in the brothels and drinking houses. Virtue you will meet in the temple, the forum and the senate house, standing before the walls, stained with dust, with callused hands; Pleasure you will find lurking and hanging around the shadows, round the baths and saunas and places that fear the aedile (a magistrate), soft and gutless, soaked in liquor and perfume, pale and plastered with the make-up and medicaments of the funeral parlour.[5]

We create from this a texture to Roman urbanism that contrasts vice in the backstreets with virtue in the forum.[6] In other words, we set out a fundamentally Stoic view of the city in which pleasure is marginalized or seen as a vice in our attempt to counter the Epicurean argument that pleasure was a primary motivation of itself.

Developing the City of Rome as a Pleasurescape – from Julius Caesar to Augustus

Julius Caesar was an Epicurean – that seems clear.[7] As such, the concept of pleasure can be utilized to comprehend his various schemes to develop the city of Rome. The provision of pleasure was a good of itself and a good to be shared. How that included the built environment is made clear for us by Cicero in his hostile discourse attacking Epicurean thinking: "Familiarity can make us fall in love with particular locations, temples and cities; gymnasia and playing fields; horses and dogs; displays of fighting and hunting."[8] The combination here points to place, architecture, and the activities associated with young men.[9] Yet, it is the provision of pleasure that underwrites the lives of these young men and, as we will see, it is precisely in the development of the city by professed Epicureans that we may better understand the focus of that development in the playing field of the young: the Campus Martius in Rome.

The projects of Julius Caesar, many of which were completed by his successor Octavian (renamed Augustus in 27 BCE), can be seen to both adorn the city and make it more convenient for urban living.[10] Caesar planned the construction of a new theatre to hold a larger audience, new libraries to be open to the public, and the reconfiguration of the Circus Maximus. He also planned to divert the river Tiber to relieve flooding, but the project was never concluded and floods continued to be a pain that Rome's citizens regularly endured.[11]

Adornment of the city was vital for the construction of a city of pleasure that included buildings for the public. A feature of this new urbanism was the portico or colonnade, a shady space for strolling and repose with laws to ensure that the portico remained repaired and open to the public. Shade was a vital quality of this new urbanism: the gladiatorial games that were held in the Forum included an awning of silk to shade spectators.[12] The new Forum with its Temple of Venus Victrix featured extensive colonnades, as did the Saepta on the Campus Martius – all these structures were creating shaded spaces and a haptic cityscape, in which inhabitants could remain cool. Significantly, Seneca was to characterize the Epicureans as an effeminate, shade-loving clan of philosophizing banqueters.[13]

1 Cicero's *On Moral Ends* (De Finibus) is the major source for both understanding and critiquing Epicurean philosophy in ancient Rome. There are numerous editions and translations available, but for this paper I refer readers to J. Annas (ed.), *Cicero: On Moral Ends* (Cambridge: Cambridge University Press, 2001).

2 Ibid., 1.37, 2.90, 3.17.

3 D. Scott, "Epicurean Illusions," *Classical Quarterly* 39 (1989): 360–74; see J. Brunschwig, "The Cradle Argument in Epicureanism and Stoicism," in M. Schofield and G. Striker (eds) *The Norms of Nature* (Cambridge: Cambridge University Press, 1986), 115–28.

4 L. Mumford, *The City in History* (London: Penguin, 1961), 239–81.

5 Translation from A. Wallace-Hadrill, "Public Honour and Private Shame: The Urban Texture of Pompeii," in T.J. Cornell and K. Lomas (eds) *Urban Society in Roman Italy* (London: University College London Press, 1995), 39–62 for discussion.

6 R. Laurence, *Roman Pompeii: Space and Society*, 2nd edition (Abingdon: Routledge, 2007), 167.

7 F.C. Bourne, "Caesar the Epicurean," *Classical World* 70 (1977): 417–32.

8 Cicero, *On Moral Ends*, 1.69.

9 The latter were avoided by many of the elite (in opposition to pleasure), who fled the city for their villas once the games began: ibid., 3.8.

10 Suetonius, *Life of Deified Julius*, 44 and *Life of Deified Augustus*, 28–30. For a synopsis of Caesar's projects see S.L. Dyson, *Rome: A Living Portrait of an Ancient City* (Baltimore: Johns Hopkins, 2010), 107–14.

11 G. Aldrete, *Floods of the Tiber in Ancient Rome* (Baltimore: Johns Hopkins, 2007).

12 Dio Cassius, *History of Rome*, 43.24.

13 Seneca, *On Benefits*, 4.1.13.

14 Most recently, L. Haselberger, "Urbem Adornare: Rome's Urban Metamorphosis under Augustus," *Journal of Roman Archaeology Supplement* 64 (2007).

15 For conception of built environment stimulating thoughts of 'great men,' see Cicero, *On Moral Ends*, 5.4 in context of Athens.

16 For power over nature, see N. Purcell, "Rome and its Development under Augustus and his Successors," in A.K. Bowman, E. Champlin, and A. Lintott (eds) *The Cambridge Ancient History* (second edition) Volume X: *The Augustan Empire, 43 BC – AD 69* (Cambridge: Cambridge University Press, 1996), 782–811.

17 Figures from D. Favro, *The Urban Image of Augustan Rome* (New York: Cambridge University Press, 1996), 171.

18 Strabo, *The Geography*, 5.3–8.

19 Ovid, *Letters from Pontus*, 1.8.33–8.

20 M. Carroll, *Earthly Paradises: Ancient Gardens in History and Archaeology* (London: British Museum Press, 2003), 29–31.

21 Plutarch, *Life of Lucullus*, 38–42.

22 Pliny, *Natural History*, 19, 50–9.

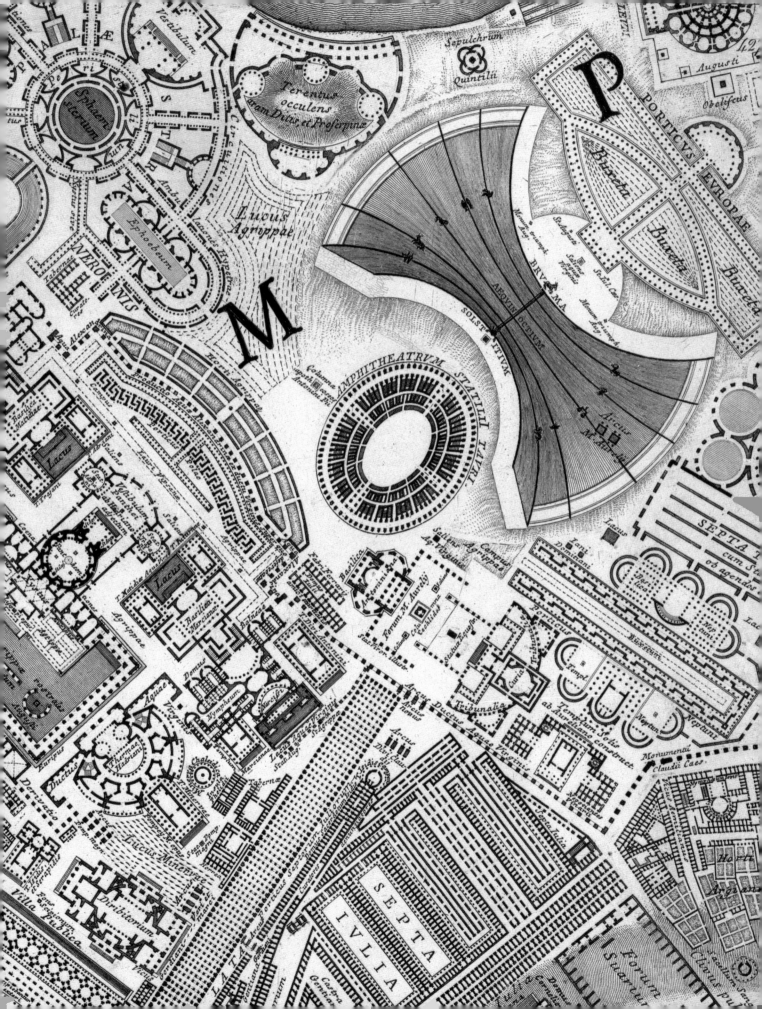

Julius Caesar's successor Augustus is seen in ancient literature as being responsible for Rome's adornment, yet modern writing links this adornment to the politics of shifting from republic to monarchy without really considering the use-value of these new urban landscapes.[14] The shift from an urban center revolving round the Forum to the exercise field of the Campus Martius becoming the primary place of adornment (with its new Baths of Agrippa, flowing water, porticoes and shade, as well as the Pantheon and gardens) was a new form of urbanism that was fundamentally created for pleasure rather than utility. Its creation, I wish to suggest, lies in Epicurean philosophy and a conception of pleasure that was haptic rather than based on virtue or recognition of achievements. This was a place for pleasure, with buildings that reminded the inhabitants of those who had built them and provided this new form of urbanism – Augustus and his family.[15] This new urban landscape might emphasize its creators' power over nature, but also there was a stress on the creation of a landscape that was pleasing: a pleasurescape.[16] Within this urban-scape, we can identify discrete units such as the Saepta, covering 37,200 square meters, or the Porticus of Octavia, containing an area of 15,708 square meters that would dwarf the Forum of Augustus at a mere 10,625 square meters. The point is that the spaces for pleasure and enjoyment dwarfed the spaces of virtue.[17] It is also the landscape of the Campus Martius that fills the page of Strabo the Geographer's account of the city, in which the Fora receive but a brief mention.[18] The Campus Martius, with its views over gardens, lakes, and water-channels, is seen by Strabo as an antidote to the utilitarianism of earlier times in Rome.[19]

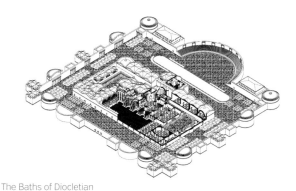

The Baths of Diocletian

Rome – the Garden City?

There are two urban-scapes in ancient Rome that provide vivid contradictory images for those who inhabit modern Western cities. One image is the familiar one, much written about, that arises from Juvenal's *Satire III*; it is a picture of crowded apartment blocks, collapsing buildings, urban destitution, and poor sanitation. The other image is of a city surrounded by pleasure parks with architectural elements that mirror the format found in the cities of the Hellenistic world, such as Athens and Alexandria. Epicurus and Plato both owned gardens in Athens and the main gymnasia were associated with gardens beyond the walls of the city of Athens, familiar to many Romans who had traveled to Athens for study in their youth.[20] What was created in Rome was a Hellenistic urban form of high-density apartment blocks, with large palaces and pleasure gardens on the surrounding hills for the elite. These included architecture in the form of porticoes, not dissimilar to the gymnasia of the Greek city equated by some Romans with luxury, pleasure, and vice.[21] However, in terms of urban form, the garden, with its architecture of monumental shade and vast variety of plants, was very much a feature of the landscape of ancient Rome. It is the contrast, as ever, to the public spaces of government and political competition – the virtue of the Forum found in Stoic thought.

Not surprisingly, Roman authors could identify the originator of these landscapes in the garden of Epicurus.[22] This has led modern writers to suggest that the garden was a place in which the Forum might be denied, shifting this discussion into the realm of the realities of power in the final decades of the Roman Republic (60–44BC).[23] Instead, we should see these pleasure gardens of the rich (that could be opened to the public) as central to the urban landscape of Rome. Stepping back from the Stoic v. Epicurean dialogues, we can find plenty of Romans seeking to own and develop gardens and also to use them as public amenities for the mass banquets given to the urban plebs.[24]

There were some 70 parks or gardens (*horti*) in Rome named after leading citizens and made available to the people of Rome for entertainment and strolling (*ambulatio*). The action of walking and thinking is deeply entrenched in Roman culture, but care was needed to ensure that you did not dress and walk like a Greek – a sign of effeminacy.[25] The major gardens of Rome were places in which one walked to be seen by the public – unlike the villa gardens of the elite in the suburbs and near the small towns of Rome's hinterland. There was a need for a Stoic, such as Seneca, to walk in a way that revealed their virtue or Stoic nature.[26] Both gardens and porticoes were associated with a different kind of walking from that found in the street – it was walking for leisure, rather than purpose (a kinetic form associated with streets and fora).[27]

Within the public gardens existed a sophisticated and cared-for landscape, with gardeners capable of creating topiary from cypress in shapes of fleets of ships and hunting scenes.[28] The major porticoes, such as that of Octavia, held enclosed gardens, while the Campus Martius featured both enclosed gardens and a larger landscape of grass and gardens. The experience of this landscape was one of buildings framed by vegetation and, once inside a portico, vegetation framed by a building. The construction of these artificial gardens transformed the urban experience; as Horace notes in his *Satires*, a gloomy walk on Rome's Servian Wall could be transformed into a walk in the sun with a view across a vast landscape of the city.[29]

Above: Colonnades of St. Peters

The Bathing Pool by Hubert Robert

The Possibility of an Urban History of Pleasure

The mismatch between the landscape produced in Rome and the Stoic view of the city with which we began points to a divergence of what was experienced in Rome and what was written about the city. The Stoic viewpoint dominates the textual evidence, but when we read the city in terms of volumes of space given over to pleasure, it outstrips the spaces the Stoics associate with virtue. Stoicism was fundamentally a preserve of a distinctive, elite cultural set of values that separated themselves from both luxury and the plebs. The other side of Stoic view was one of pleasure-seeking Epicureans and the plebs, who benefitted from the public provision of games, dinners, baths, and so on. Stoicism denies the utility or use-value of the provision of pleasure to the people of Rome, which is also a view reflected in modern writing on ancient Rome. There is a sense in which modern writers cannot accept that cities, including Rome, were created and managed to deliver pleasure to their citizens, just as a slave was there to enable a lifestyle of pleasure, rather than work, for the elite. This parallels, perhaps, the modern conceit that cities are not about consumption, and every effort is made to divert us from this realization through aligning consumption to cultural activities.[30]

There is a sense by which the contemporary focus on 'austerity' in the face of the world economic crisis is re-creating a 19th-century emphasis on enjoyment through toil. The idea that the urban environment might be a thing of leisure, or even pleasure, is avoided. Cultural assets (museums and galleries) are not safe from the ideologies associated with austerity. Instead, museums and galleries are expected to make money, or pay for themselves, within this conception of purpose. The idea that people may gain pleasure or knowledge from such venues is not discussed. This is the new Stoicism of Europe of the 21st century. Austerity needs to be resisted: we wish to shift the debate of cultural utility away from simplistic notions of cost to other values, including the pleasure gained from living within a vibrant cultural city in urban redevelopment. Part of that pleasure is the contrast between the spaces of inhabitation and work and the spaces of entertainment and leisure. The contrast to ancient Rome could not be starker. The dynamic of the relationship between spaces of utility and pleasure in ancient Rome probably has greater value than the contrast between public and private space, which was legally based, or rural and urban, which is proved false through the development of Rome as an urban form of parklands with high-density habitation.

The possibility of a city based around the creation of spaces for enjoyment was explored in a recently published manuscript written by Henri Lefebvre in the 1970s.[31] It is striking, reading this book, that in ancient Rome so much of its surface area was devoted to the creation of enjoyment with a much smaller area devoted to the pursuit of virtue (the fora). The porticoes and gardens associated with pleasure, haptic walking, and thought were spaces that could have been appropriated by the Stoics. Their use, unlike the amphitheater or circus, was subject to redefinition—the greatest change being the access to these spaces by the wider public—but the organization of enjoyment within them was focused on the provision of pleasure, particularly during the reign of Nero.[32]

It is difficult to know whether this landscape of pleasure in ancient Rome was spontaneous or a commodity created through the emperor's power, but what is certain is that there was a sensory landscape that was designed to alleviate pain and provide the population with pleasure. If we accept the argument that Rome is an origin point for all cities that came after it,[33] then we need to reconnect the architecture of today to the actual landscape of ancient Rome, in which architecture produced spaces of pleasure that dominated the city.

23 Wallace-Hadrill, "Public Honour and Private Shame," 5–6.

24 For discussion of opening gardens to the public and banquets, see J.H. D'Arms, "Between public and private: the Epulum Publicum and Caesar's Horti Trans Tiberim," in M. Cima and E. La Rocca (eds), *Horti Romani* (Rome: L'Erma di Bretschneider, 1998), 33–43.

25 T.M. O'Sullivan, *Walking in Roman Culture* (Cambridge: Cambridge University Press, 2011), 34–50.

26 Ibid., 41–46.

27 E. Macaulay-Lewis, "The City in Motion: Walking for Transport and Leisure in the City of Rome," in R. Laurence & D. Newsome (eds) *Rome, Ostia, Pompeii: Movement and Space* (Oxford: Oxford University Press, 2011), 262–89.

28 P. Grimal, *Les Jardins Romains* (Paris: Presses Universitaires de France, 1969), 107–64 for named gardens; 87–98 for discussion of topiary.

29 Horace, *Satires*, 1.8; see also T.P. Wiseman, "A Stroll on the Rampart," in *Horti Romani*, 13–22.

30 S. Miles, *Spaces for Consumption: Pleasure and Placelessness in the Post-Industrial City* (Sage: Los Angeles, 2010), 4.

31 H. Lefebvre, *Toward an Architecture of Enjoyment* (Minneapolis: University of Minnesota Press, 2014).

32 E. Champlin, *Nero* (Cambridge: Belknap Press, 2003) provides an overview of pleasure provision in the Campus Martius and ultimately in the Golden House.

33 A. Graafland and C. Bos, "A Conversation with Rem Koolhaas," in M. Speaks (ed.), *The Critical Landscape* (Rotterdam: 010 Publishers, 1996), recognised also by Lefebvre, *Toward an Architecture of Enjoyment*, ch. 11 discussing the Baths of Diocletian as a space of pleasure.

MARK KINGWELL
URBAN PLEASURES

00:18

00:21

00:24

00:27

Mark Kingwell is a Professor of Philosophy at the University of Toronto and a contributing editor of *Harper's Magazine* in New York. He is the author or co-author of 17 books of political, cultural, and aesthetic theory, including *Better Living* (1998), *The World We Want* (2000), *Concrete Reveries* (2008), and *Glenn Gould* (2009). His articles on politics, architecture, and art have appeared both in academic journals and also mainstream publications, such as *Harper's, The New York Times, The Wall Street Journal*, and *The Guardian*. Mark has held visiting posts at Cambridge University, the University of California, Berkeley, and the City University of New York, where he was the Weissman Distinguished Visiting Professor of Humanities. His most recent book is a collection of political essays, *Unruly Voices* (2012).

➕ PHILOSOPHY

Framed Residential View

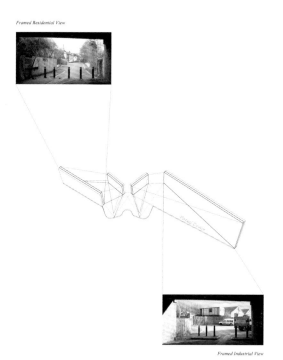

Framed Industrial View

The Situationist Drawing Device: The device enables each eye's retina to receive different views that blur into each other.

"In the city there's a thousand things I want to say to you.
But whenever I approach you, you make me look a fool."
The Jam, "In The City" (1977)

Gift

In economic jargon, an externality is any cost or benefit that is experienced outside of a contract. Urban life, which is only ever partially tamed by explicit transaction, is full of them. Uncompensated costs are negative externalities: noise, pollution, body contact on the subway, long lines at the baseball game beer stand. Unexpected benefits are positive externalities: the sex appeal of passing strangers, the excitement of a neon-splashed downtown square, all the incidental stimulation that Georg Simmel—writing in 1903—associated with "the metropolitan attitude."[1]

"The psychological foundation, upon which the metropolitan individuality is erected," he wrote, "is the intensification of emotional life due to the swift and continuous shift of external and internal stimuli...the rapid telescoping of changing images, pronounced differences within what is grasped at a single glance, the unexpectedness of violent stimuli."[2] This violence occurs, indeed, "with every crossing of the street, with the tempo and multiplicity of economic, occupational and social life."[3] To cope with this onslaught, the metropolitan mind adopts a "blasé outlook," a "relentless matter-of-factness" of been-there, done-that cool.[4]

Meanwhile, every interaction in the city seeks to reduce any particularity to the 'rational' uniform calculability of transaction, as money smoothes down the differences between things, or 'reserve' the interactions between people – or, indeed, the way the then newly ubiquitous pocket watches made all time the same unit-based flow. "If all the watches in Berlin suddenly went wrong in different ways even only as much as an hour, its entire commercial and economic life would be derailed for some time." Thus, Simmel concludes, "the most banal externalities," such as watches, "are, in the last analysis, bound up with the final decisions concerning the meaning and the style of life."[5]

But Simmel is too deterministic, and he gives away the game to 'rational' capitalism too easily. Another way to think of externalities is this: they are gifts, unrequested and unrequited pleasures descending upon us without warning or price. They are, indeed, beyond or behind the very idea of transaction, not just external to it. A gift offers an alternative, potentially critical scale of value independent of the world in which all things and experiences must have a price. You can buy a gift, perhaps, but you cannot constrain its ability to give any more than the value of a work of art is reducible to its price.[6]

The gift of the city is the gift of democratic pleasure, a constantly renewed sense of open possibility and playful engagement between self and other. If that sounds too abstract, let me add some concreteness to the point by describing my walk yesterday evening.

I was on my way to meet an old friend for a drink. He is my oldest friend, in the sense that he is someone I have known for three decades and we still feel the same pleasure in each other's company as we did during college in the 1980s. In the manner of Heidegger's "horizon of concern," I was already in a sense engaged with him even as I left my office.[7] Anticipatory resoluteness! I decided to walk.

Because I now teach at the same university where I was an undergraduate, the streets of downtown Toronto are for me layered with rich deposits of memory: some wistful and slightly tragic in the way that only the recalled loves of 19 can be; some harsh or embarrassing, according to relevant incident; some purely and simply beautiful.

First, then, through Yorkville, a self-consciously tony neighborhood of boutiques, bistros, and heavyset men smoking fat Cuban cigars on the wide terraces. There used to be a bookstore here, staffed by a woman called Gwyneth, who I was in love with, and a man called Paul, an author whose work I admired and who later became a friend and fishing buddy, until cancer took him. I remember buying a copy of a book by J.D. Salinger there 30 years ago, then walking through light snow and twinkling lights to the subway that would make its long northward journey to the dull suburb where I lived.

It was my city's version of the Salinger twilight now, I realized, the "faintly soupy quarter of an hour in New York when the street lights have just been turned on and the parking lights of cars are just getting turned on."[8] This is the scene—maybe you know the one—where Seymour tells his brother Buddy not to aim at the other kid's marble, because *aiming* means he doesn't believe in the truth of striking the marble.[9] There is the bar where I confronted my first great love and begged her to take me back. She wouldn't, but then, when I was halfway around the world, she wrote me a letter regretting it that I carried with me for two years.

Now the park where, a long time after that, I stood in the rain with another beloved who was, alas, not the woman I was married to. We stood and talked, and kissed, as the rain soaked us through. A marriage ended.

Now an old tavern, a place where they have salt shakers on the rickety tables so you can refresh your flat glass of draft beer. Summer nights here, after pickup baseball games during college years and after, arguing and flirting and dancing to The Clash and the Jackson Five. Across the road, what used to be a concert hall: Toots and the Maytals, Los Lobos, lots of local talent. Then, years later, it was a TV studio where I met a famous hockey enforcer who was the sweetest man you can imagine, and where a tall gentlemanly quarterback, also famous, offered me a lift in his convertible.

What else? The old train station that is now the largest wine and liquor store in the city. The now-abandoned offices of the publisher who accepted my first trade book, and where I dropped off the printed-out manuscript with an intense feeling of youthful triumph that would neither last nor return. The little French bakery with those inimitable ham and butter baguettes. The all-night diner where we used to go for eggs and toast after finishing production on the college newspaper. The pub that wryly commemorates a half-hearted rebellion in our peaceful, once-parochial burg: an uprising whose energy petered out with the prospect of a cold beer.

Amazingly, not a single smartphone zombie blocked my path along the way. Maybe less amazingly, at least three times I passed youngsters smoking pot in open spaces. And so, to the quiet bar where Charlie is waiting. A half hour of walking, a half century of life. The city gives us these textures, sometimes whether we like it or not.

Justice and Things

For Simmel, it seems as though everything distinctive about urban pleasure is an externality, but yet one conditioned by the dominant transactional economy. Patrick Turmel has argued, contrarily, that the problem with urban externalities is that they are unruly, as well as ubiquitous.[10] If we take the project of justice to be one in which citizens of a shared political space can make legitimate demands upon one another, including ones of redistribution, then the proliferation of externalities renders the prospect more distant.[11]

But is this correct? Suppose we view the superfluity of externalities in the city not as a problem to be solved—internalizing them, or some of them, in a just social contract—but instead as a kind of renewed opportunity for playful, spontaneous, and unplanned interaction. Now the stranger on the street is not a competitor for scarce goods within a fixed system, but rather a new player in an infinite game of free interchange.

The Situationist architect Constant Nieuwenhuys designed a city based on this concept of play. He called it New Babylon, with a deliberate wry reference to the ancient mythical city of polyglot excess. In New Babylon, citizens enact constantly renewed versions of the *dérive* advocated by Guy Debord and the other Situationist pioneers, recasting the planned routes and goal-driven byways of the city into opportunities for getting lost or finding oneself nowhere in particular. In the undirected movement of the *dérive*, one's own movements are themselves gifts of chance and randomness.[12] "In a *dérive*," Debord says, "one or more persons during a certain period drop their usual motives for movement and action, their relations, their work and leisure activities, and let themselves be drawn by the attractions of the terrain and the encounters they find there."[13]

Increasingly this is a lost art, and a diminishing possibility within the city. In part, this is because we have lost the art of becoming strange to ourselves, artfully losing control over

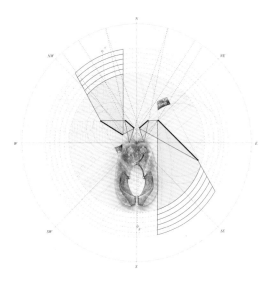

With one eye looking forward and the other looking backward, the retinal rivalry creates a new perception of the site.

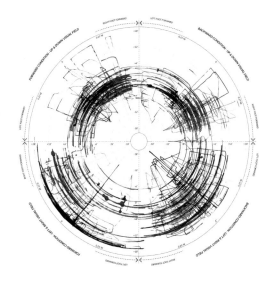

Perception Drawing: Connected to various parts of the body, the device also records the bodily movement as one navigates the city with a retinal rivalry vision.

the world and our relation to it. Public action, once considered the highest expression of human life in what Hannah Arendt called "the space of appearances," is swapped out for willed isolation and technological swaddling of every imaginable kind.[14]

Consider, for example, the growing trend of the internet of things (IoT), wherein even the most banal appliance or material feature of everyday life will be linked with monitoring and surveillance technology, instantly communicating one with another. Simmel was correct about watches: they tell time, and so reinforce the tyranny of mathesis that is the modern time standard. But at least with watches we know what they do, and why. In the IoT, our toasters and washing machines, our vehicles and clothes, become part of a comprehensive network of information sharing that works, as with everything else associated with the internet, to reinforce corporate ownership. "The Internet of Things will connect every thing with everyone in an integrated global network," confidently predicts Jeremy Rifkin. "People, machines, natural resources, production lines, logistics networks, consumption habits, recycling flows, and virtually every other aspect of economic and social life will be linked via sensors and software to the IoT platform, continually feeding Big Data to every node—businesses, homes, vehicles—moment to moment, in real time." The result will be a post-capitalist economy in which coordinated systems "dramatically increase productivity, and reduce the marginal cost of producing a full range of goods and services to near zero across the entire economy."[15]

Really? Surely we have good reason to doubt not just the viability but also the positive effects of any real-world version of the IoT. In truth, under this new global-capital space-time regime—for that is what platform-feeding 'nodes' amount to—the imperatives of unwanted convenience (why read a recipe from a book when you can have it read to you by your stove?) will merely reinforce an enmeshment with state institutions, private firms, and transnational revenue streams. One CEO, quoted in a news story on some of the coming advances in appliances, let slip the true message of the IoT: "It can be hard to explain to consumers all the promise of a Web-connected dishwasher or washing machine, but...they're inevitable."[16] Of course they are! That's what new devices and upgraded models always are, the *avatars of inevitability*.

In this world of total control, the 24/7 availability of the person to the demands of transactions and devices, we are all seclusion but zero privacy. The essential insight about individual life—that its right to privacy is itself an achievement of public discourse—is obscured by use-value and disposability in all things. That includes, of course, ourselves. Now we consume not merely goods and services, or even experiences and desires, but the very idea of the self, cannibalized from within under the twinned signs of empty pleasure and technological mastery. "A 24/7 environment has the semblance of a social world," the critic Jonathan Crary writes, "but it is actually a non-social model of machinic performance and a suspension of living that does not disclose the human cost required to sustain its effectiveness."[17]

Time itself has once more altered shape, now beyond the calculability and uniformity noted by Simmel. 24/7 time, Crary argues, "must be distinguished from what Lukács and others in the early 20th century identified as the empty, homogenous time of modernity, the metric or calendar time of nations, of finance and industry...What is new is the sweeping abandonment of the pretence that time is coupled to any long-term undertakings, even to fantasies of 'progress' or development."[18]

Note the irony: once *sleep* was figured as the visage of drugged complacency, a trope of ideological self-dupery found in everything from Marx's notion of false consciousness to the resistance cry that features in John Carpenter's 1988 ideological horror film *They Live*–a favorite of Slavoj Zizek–in which alien invaders tame susceptible earthlings by feeding them advertising slogans and consumer products ("They live, we sleep!"). Now, sleep is the last line of resistance against the relentless reach of time-bending technological immersion. But as so often occurs, the ideological enemy works by stealth. "24/7 is a time of indifference," Crary notes, "against which the fragility of human life is increasingly inadequate and within which sleep has no necessity or inevitability."[19]

An old complaint, even if presented in new terms. Compare, for example, the critic Northrop Frye, writing in 1967 about the modern city. "To the modern imagination the city becomes increasingly something hideous and nightmarish, the *fourmillante cité* of Baudelaire, the 'unreal city' of Eliot's *Waste Land*, the *ville tentaculaire* of Verhaeren," Frye notes. "No longer a community, it seems more like a community turned inside out, with its expressways taking its thousands of self-enclosed nomadic units in a headlong flight into greater solitude, ants in the body of a dying dragon, breathing its polluted air and passing its polluted water."[20] And in this nightmarish city, the problems of time and privacy are already inscribed, even if they have not yet reached the 24/7 endgame. "The last stand of privacy has always been, traditionally, the inner mind," Frye argues. "It is quite possible however for communications media, especially the newer electronic ones, to break down the associative structures of the inner mind and replace them by the prefabricated structures of the media."[21] *They live, we dream while awake!* And so: "A society controlled by their slogans and exhortations would be introverted, because nobody would be saying anything; there would only be echo, and Echo was the mistress of Narcissus."[22]

The point is not to condemn individual users, however; and the charge of narcissism is now no more than a part of the ritual exchange of hollowed-out social discourse, easily made and just as easily dismissed. No, the point is to give some urgency to the very idea of pleasure. Get lost in the city, my friends! Get lost to yourself and your routine desires! Become a stranger to yourself, and then engage with the strangers who walk, zombie-fashion, along our shared city streets. This is not New Babylon–which perhaps imagines more spontaneity than some of us could easily stand–but it is the unexpected gift of genuine newness, rather than the pre-packaged novelties of techno-inevitability. The pleasures to be gained thereby will forever render the other kind into a kind of bad dream, time spent gazing at a hypnotic series of screens, revealed to be no more than funhouse mirrors – but with elaborate profit structures attached to them.

Out of the funhouse, into the sun! And then, when we choose, the blessed refuge of sleep.

1 Georg Simmel, "The Metropolis and Mental Life," in Gary Bridge & Sophie Watson (eds), *The Blackwell City Reader* (Hoboken: Wiley-Blackwell, 2010).

2 Ibid., 11.

3 Ibid.

4 Ibid., 12.

5 Ibid., 13.

6 See, for example, Lewis Hyde, *The Gift: Imagination and the Erotic Life of Property* (New York: Vintage, 1979).

7 See Martin Heidegger, *Being and Time*, John Macquarrie & Edward Robinson, trans., (New York: Harper & Row, 1962), 364 ff.

8 J.D. Salinger, *Raise High the Roof Beam, Carpenters and Seymour: An Introduction* (New York: Bantam, 1965), 201.

9 Ibid., 201–3.

10 See Patrick Turmel, "The City as Public Space," in Mark Kingwell & Patrick Turmel (eds), *Rites of Way: The Politics and Poetics of Public Space* (Waterloo: Wilfrid Laurier University Press, 2009), 151–64.

11 Ibid.

12 I discuss Constant's design in relation to contemporary architecture in Kingwell, "Building Cities, Making Friends: A Meditation, in Five General Propositions," *Queen's Quarterly* 119, no. 3 (2012): 359–77.

13 From Guy Debord, "Theory of the Dérive," *Les Lèvres Nues* 9 (November 1956); reprinted in *Internationale Situationniste* 2 (December 1958); Ken Knabb, trans., is at http://www.cddc.vt.edu/sionline/si/theory.html.

14 See Hannah Arendt, *The Human Condition*, 2nd ed. (Chicago: University of Chicago Press, 1998); for deft and provocative application of Arendt's idea to architecture and urbanism, see George Baird, *The Space of Appearance* (Cambridge, MA: MIT Press, 1995).

15 Quoted in Sue Halpern, "The Creepy New Wave of the Internet," *The New York Review of Books* (20 November 2014). The article reviews books about the IoT phenomenon by Rifkin, David Rose, Robert Scobie and Shel Israel, and Jim Dwyer.

16 Quoted in Scott Feschuk, *The Future and Why We Should Avoid It* (Vancouver: Douglas & McIntyre, 2014), 16.

17 Jonathan Crary, *24/7: Late Capitalism and the Ends of Sleep* (London: Verso, 2013), 9.

18 Ibid.

19 Ibid.

20 Northrop Frye, *The Modern Century* (Oxford: Oxford University Press, 1967), 37.

21 Ibid., p. 38.

22 Ibid.

RANDALL MASON
NOTES ON A CITY BUILT FOR PLEASURE

AERO VIEW OF

ATLANTIC CITY

NEW JERSEY
1909

> [S]o nearly, dearly and serenely is [Atlantic City] now civilized—once wild and savage retreat, connected with all our thoughts of hot weather pleasures—all our dreams of summer joy, that the history here presented will undoubtedly be read by old and young—by saint and sage—by cleric and disciple—for it is, at once, the record of home life and high life, of low life and middle life—the story of joys, pleasures and pastimes—of happy fights with foaming waves—of long-loved walks and lovely drives—all of which are, and have been the product of that mighty and conquering genius, known to us all by the name of American enterprise.[1]

Randall Mason PhD, FAAR, is a geographer and planner by training, born and raised in Atlantic City and Brigantine on the Jersey coast. He is Associate Professor and Chair of the Graduate Program in Historic Preservation at the University of Pennsylvania, and Executive Director of the University of Pennsylvania School of Design's 'clinical' practice arm, PennPraxis.

✚ HISTORIC PRESERVATION

Atlantic City makes for a good story, and it's all about pleasure. The city's creation is a classic American tale of booster-driven urban invention in which the main character, the city itself, careens between ruthless exploitation for profit and exuberant celebration of abundant natural resources or subtle landscape. In both of these modes, in the 19th century as today, pleasure is central to the city's narrative and to its experience. Atlantic City was designed to deliver pleasure.

In one respect Atlantic City is a singular place: the pioneering mass seaside resort renowned and romanticized as "the World's Playground" and dramatized in HBO's recent *Boardwalk Empire* series. In deeper regard, though, Atlantic City is a typical American place: a single-purpose city driven by industry, organized around class and racial distinctions, buffeted by boom-and-bust cycles – hitting it big in the era of railroad tourism and hitting rock bottom (recently) in the era of casino gambling. It is a city at once dependent on the charms and lures of its natural setting and mindlessly ignorant and destructive of its deeper nature.

Created in the 1850s, Atlantic City was sited in more or less virgin, uninhabited landscape on a barrier island on the southern New Jersey coast. Here, flat, thin islands with gently sloping beaches, dune sets, and scrubby uplands a few meters in elevation are separated from the mainland by miles of open bay and low tidal marshes. This part of the coast was exceedingly marginal until railroad connections made it central to the East Coast conurbation.

The American landscape narrative of the last third of the 19th century was specialization – new, specialized landscapes created for the burgeoning, differentiated economy and the new social worlds and cultural practices that resulted. As a purpose-built seaside resort, Atlantic City epitomized this. It introduced new building types (a variety of new hotel types, dense blocks of cottages, amusement piers, and the Boardwalk) and aesthetic experiences enabled by the reshuffling of public and private spaces and behavioral norms (flirting on the beach, cruising the speakeasies, promenading on the Boardwalk, the anonymity of being away from the prying eyes of home and polite society). Atlantic City was imagined and invented as an unproductive place. Nothing is made there – only experiences, either pleasurable or healthful, but always profitable. It is a city built for the sale and consumption of pleasure.

The forms of pleasure available for consumption in Atlantic City have changed over time, and at any given moment spanned the licit and the illicit: from the Victorian heyday and Prohibition-era naughtiness to contemporary casino glitz. The Boardwalk, which mediates city and sea, serves as the principal public space – a threshold between the commercial pleasures of the city and the bodily pleasures of sea-bathing. It is central to the city's soul and its landscape. First built in the 1870s, it has been destroyed, rebuilt, and even relocated multiple times, buffeted by storms and by the changing economies of pleasure (from restaurants and bathhouses to massive casino complexes). Having changed form so often, yet remaining geographically and psychically central to the place, the Boardwalk seems an American incarnation of Asian temples like the Japanese Shinto Ise Shrine – ritualistically rebuilt in ways that reinforce its centrality and meaning through time.

Until the 1870s, visitors to the shore consumed the healthful seaside air but barely touched the sand, and mostly stayed out of the water. The Boardwalk, when first built, represented a halting step toward the surf. People were splashing by the 1880s, at first as a health cure, with measured doses of pleasure administered to restore what bodily and mental costs had been exacted by the frenetic, industrialized life back home. This move into the waves, clothed in flannel swimsuits and chaste behavior at first, opened the door to other pleasures. Pleasures more transcendent than the salacious ones dramatized by *Boardwalk Empire* – the bodily pleasures of mucking around in nature itself, in sand, water, mud, waves, dunes, grass, burrs, seaweed.

What does Atlantic City feel like? The boards underfoot; gentle sloping beaches of hot sand to a surf of mostly kid-sized waves rolling over your feet while you contemplate the endless horizon and some invisible distant shore. The beach gives one license to be un-serious and un-productive. What comfort in remembering these bodily pleasures at a distance: the sun's warmth and crust of salt on your skin from a warm afternoon on the beach seems warmer, saltier, sweeter from my desk in Philadelphia on a cold fall day. These are the more lasting pleasures.

In a world where landscape is so overwhelmingly framed by consumption and other modes of performance, Atlantic City and its coastal landscape present us a conundrum of a useful sort – a place where it is possible to consume the totally packaged, estranged pleasure of casinos (eyes on the dollar signs), or the bodily, unscripted pleasures of immersing oneself in the surf, daydreaming, eyes on the horizon.

We talk a lot about aesthetics in the design fields, but rarely do we consider all that this means and how transformative a set of perspectives it can lend to the typical, public discourses about design and environment. Aesthetics invoke the senses. All of them. And not just as consumed experience, but as bodily experience. Our society obsesses mostly about money, about style, about social positioning. We are so wrapped up in "conspicuous consumption" and "invidious comparison" (Thorstein Veblen nailed this more than a century ago[2]) that we fail to sense and experience deeply the environments in which we wrap ourselves. The Jersey coast, in its several historical and contemporary versions, provides relief from this mundane, endless, and mostly meaningless talk.

1 R.L. Carnesworth, *Atlantic City: Its Early and Modern History* (Philadelphia: W.C. Harris and Co., 1868), 6–7.

2 Thorstein Veblen, *Theory of the Leisure Class* (New York: Penguin Books, 1994).

JOSEPHINE KANE
DREAM

Josephine Kane is the British Academy Post Doctoral Fellow in the Department of Architecture at the University of Westminster, London. Trained as a design historian, her special interest is the relationship between the experience of pleasure, modernity, and the architectural landscape in 19th- and 20th-century Britain. Her book *The Architecture of Pleasure* (2013) presents early amusement parks, and the mechanical thrill rides they contained, as a key component in the experience of urban modernity. Kane is currently collaborating on a new interdisciplinary project exploring vertigo and the city, and is a general editor of *Architectural Histories: The Open Access Journal of the European Architectural History Network*.

✚ DESIGN HISTORY, SOCIOLOGY, CULTURAL STUDIES

London is in the throes of a pleasure revival. Its major landmarks and public spaces are being transformed by a growing appetite for new and thrilling ways to consume the urban environment. The London Eye, a 135-meter revolving observation wheel on the South Bank, offers spectacular panoramic views to nearly four million passengers each year. High-speed powerboats provide river tours of the capital with a white-knuckle twist. The O2 Arena in Greenwich invites us to 'clip on' and climb a vertigo-inducing suspended track stretching up and over its enormous domed canopy. At the Olympic Park, the looping red tower of Anish Kapoor's ArcelorMittal Orbit blurs the line between sculpture and thrill ride. And, most recently, on Tower Bridge itself—one of London's most iconic structures—engineered glass floors have been inserted into a high-level walkway, creating the giddying illusion of walking on air, 42 meters above the swirling river and the world-famous bridge below.

The proliferation of urban novelties in London and other cities reveals a collective desire for a more embodied experience of the modern city, for technological multisensory spectacles, which might reconnect us emotionally to a landscape often characterized as anonymous or dehumanized. But the idea of the city as technological playground has roots that stretch beyond Rem Koolhaas' thrilling Manhattanism or Cedric Price's Fun Palace. Londoners at the turn of the 20th century were no less hungry for exhilarating high-tech sensations; but, rather than delight in playful interventions in the everyday urban environment, they flocked to a new kind of purpose-built pleasurescape: the amusement park.

The early amusement parks, which appeared at exhibition sites and pleasure grounds around the country in the early 1900s, were enclosed sites combining thrill rides with the most popular entertainments of the day. Inspired by the pioneering parks at New York's Coney Island, these engineered otherworlds were designed to transport visitors away from the blandness of working life, to relax social etiquettes, and to encourage everyone to be spendthrifts for the day. The appeal of kinesthetic pleasures—of giant thrill machines, fast-flowing crowds, and spectacular landscapes—transcended age,

CITY

LONDON'S PLEASURESCAPES

gender, and class boundaries, attracting people from all walks of life in vast numbers. Between 1900 and 1939, over 40 major parks operated across Britain and, by the outbreak of World War II, millions visited these sites each year.

In London, almost no physical trace of the golden age of British amusement parks survives, but the ghost of pleasures past manifests in some intriguing ways. The forgotten parks at Earl's Court, Olympia, Crystal Palace, Battersea, and Wembley forged new ideas about modern pleasure that have been hugely influential. The rise (and fall) of these great urban amusements resonates in the current enthusiasm for architectural pleasure-seeking in the city, but the relationship is not straightforward. Both belong to a much older story about the shifting fortunes of pleasure—and leisure—since the Industrial Revolution.

Amusement Park: Rise & Fall

London's first purpose-built amusement park opened in 1908, conceived as a light-hearted sideline for visitors to Imre Kiralfy's new exhibition ground at White City, Shepherds Bush. In fact, the park's spectacular rides came to dominate the whole site and were reproduced in countless postcards and souvenirs. Descriptions of the 'mechanical marvels' dominated the press. Readers of *The Times* were informed of long queues for the Flip Flap—an extraordinary ride with gigantic steel arms carrying passengers back and forth in a 200-foot arc—and of the endless cars crawling to the top of the Spiral Railway rollercoaster before "roaring and rattling, round and round to the bottom."[1] The annual exhibitions held

at White City were visited by millions, but it was the amusement park that captured the public imagination.[2]

White City exploited a growing market for mechanical amusements in London, epitomized by attractions such as the Great Wheel at Earl's Court (1896–1907) and the Topsy Turvy Railway at Crystal Palace, Sydenham, a loop-the-loop rollercoaster that claimed to have entertained over 40,000 passengers during the 1902 season.[3] But White City was London's first fully fledged amusement park, and its opening coincides with a brief but frenzied phase of investment in Coney Island-inspired ventures which reached far beyond the capital.

Just as riding a bicycle or shopping in a department store were identified as activities unique to the modern age, a trip to an amusement park became one way in which Edwardians across Britain could experience 'being modern.' The shock of modernity was experienced quite literally through a host of rides designed to bump, shake, and startle the body in novel and apparently enjoyable ways. The exhilaration associated with new technologies of speed, such as the motorcar and aeroplane, were well beyond the reach of all but the wealthiest few. By providing machine simulations of the latest modern wonders, the amusement parks inaugurated a socially inclusive culture of mechanized thrill-seeking, which continues to thrive today in endless variations.

The appeal of the parks continued to grow in the interwar years, with Londoners travelling out to the nearest seaside resorts for days spent at the new parks at Dreamland, Margate, and the Kursaal in Southend. However, World War II marked a watershed and the postwar era saw what would be London's last great amusement park. In 1951, the Festival of Britain featured a pleasure garden with classic thrill rides–including a Water Chute and Big Dipper–installed alongside themed landscapes and nostalgic novelties. The amusement park outlived the Festival, remaining open throughout the 1960s and early 1970s.[4]

As new forms of entertainment emerged, Battersea–like parks around the country–struggled to substantiate their claims of cutting-edge modernity. Many of the technological pleasures popularized by the early parks (flying, driving, and foreign travel) shifted from the world of public entertainment into the realm of private consumption. More people were able to afford first-hand experience of modern pleasures in the second half of the century, and so the demand for simulations of new technologies and exotic locations began to fade. Respectable pleasures were increasingly sought in personal consumption – of food, holidays, films, cars, and other newly available commodities.

A resurgence of debate about the effects of mechanized amusement sealed the fate of the amusement park. Influential cultural commentators such as Richard Hoggart warned of a new degenerate breed of working-class youth, "the hedonistic but passive barbarian," who formed the target audience for mass entertainment.[5] Filmmaker Lindsay Anderson's *O Dreamland* (1953) depicts the cultural impoverishment of London's working classes through a series of grim, abstracted shots of Dreamland amusement park, and reflected a growing chorus of concern.[6] Seaside parks faced dwindling numbers of domestic holidaymakers in the postwar period and, with fewer profits to reinvest in rides and facilities, the amusement park industry as a whole went into decline.

The final blow came in 1972, when Battersea amusement park closed after a mechanical failure on the Big Dipper caused multiple fatalities. The reputation of the parks never really recovered and the Battersea tragedy signaled the end of an era. Across the country, wooden rollercoasters were demolished and major parks were forced to shut down.

The kinesthetic pleasures made popular by early amusement parks were embraced and reinvigorated in the 1980s and 1990s by a new generation of out-of-town, Disney-inspired theme parks in Britain. These continue to offer a sanitized, family-friendly version of the technology-for-fun formula, encouraging visitors to identify themselves as consumers of modern leisure. The shift from public pleasure-seeker to leisure consumer suggests a momentous cultural transformation has been played out in the built environment over the last century.

The fact that Westfield, London's first mega-mall, now straddles the 40-acre site once occupied by White City's ground-breaking amusement park reflects this wider process. The site's reincarnation as a giant shopping and leisure complex shows how radically our conception of public pleasure has altered, and hints at a rather more complex trajectory from Edwardian rollercoasters to today's urban thrills than at first appears.

The Pleasure Problem

Leisure, so the dictionary tells us, refers to activity outside work. To be 'at leisure' is to have time at one's disposal, free from occupation. The term has specific associations with class and aspirational social practices, often in a collective sense (the 'leisured classes'). Pleasure, on the other hand, is rooted in the phenomenological. It is the "condition or sensation induced by the experience or anticipation of what is felt to be good or desirable; a feeling of happy satisfaction or enjoyment; delight, gratification. Opposed to pain."[7] Implicit within these definitions is a distinction between *practice and experience*: leisure is what you *do*, pleasure is what you *feel*. It is not surprising, then, that during the last 200 years, distinct kinds of architectural experience have been produced by these distinct ideologies. The rise and fall of urban amusement parks illustrates how the world of popular entertainment provides a point of tension between the competing regimes of pleasure and leisure.

Shared notions of what might constitute pleasurable activities were transformed by the onset of modernity. Before the 18th century, when classical philosophy and Christian theology wholly rejected the earthly pleasures of the senses, pleasure was seen as being vulgar and self-destructive, to be avoided and self-denied. During the Enlightenment, however, popular pleasure-taking was sanctioned for the first time. Influential thinkers, such as Hobbes in the 1650s and Mandeville in the early 1700s, successfully disseminated the idea that self-fulfillment, rather than denial, was a natural human instinct and could be beneficial to the national well-being. The 'new hedonism'–the moderate pursuit of pleasures–came to encompass both individual sensory gratification (drinking, eating, and sex) and more convivial practices (such as the shared enjoyment of theatre and public spectacles). The 18th-century pleasure garden embodied many of the hallmarks of this newly accepted notion of public pleasure.[8]

The early Victorians continued the legacy of moderate public pleasures–in the shape of parks, tea-drinking rituals, and a host of commercial entertainments–whilst simultaneously viewing the pleasure-seeking masses with a mixture of scorn and dread. Reacting against the excesses of their Georgian forebears, the Victorians looked upon most forms of mass merrymaking as breeding grounds for debauchery and social unrest.[9] Malthus's highly influential doctrine of 'moral restraint' (1803), for example, identified the working classes as lacking cultivation and self-discipline, regressive traits borne out by their love of 'drunkenness and dissipation.'[10] From the 1830s, the middle-class rational recreation movement sought to counter this predisposition towards dangerous bodily pleasures by

The Flip-Flap,
Franco-British Exhibition, London, 1908

329

promoting organized and edifying non-work activities.[11] And so the idea of leisure as a way of managing pleasure finds its first expression.

Simultaneously, an explosion of commercialized entertainment in industrial Britain allowed the masses to participate in a much wider range of commercial pleasure pursuits. Government authorities were anxious to regulate the new entertainment industries, whilst the entrepreneurs running them found that safe and respectable ventures were the most lucrative. By the 1890s, thanks to the mutual interests of businessmen and local authorities, the popular pleasures of circus, fairground, pub, and music hall did not seem so threatening – a shift which the early amusement parks took full advantage of.

The late 19th and early 20th centuries brought commodified, respectable public pleasures to a larger and more diverse audience than ever before. At the same time, new notions of pleasure were emerging. International exhibitions, department stores, and mechanized transport foregrounded the pleasures of visual spectacle and bodies in motion. The amusement parks combined the legacy of these 19th-century phenomena– transience, crowds, spectacle, and speed–with technologically produced multisensory experience. In doing so, they forged a new and specifically modern form of respectable pleasure.[12]

At the amusement park, the consumption of pleasure was mediated by mechanization. The 'gear and girder' aesthetic of the industrialized city was relocated to the world of recreation in the form of mechanical rides and, in particular, the rollercoaster.[13] By 1910, mechanically produced multisensory stimulation–promoted as health-giving, thrilling, transformative, and transcendent–was, for the first time, widely accepted as pleasurable.

Contemporary commentators were often bemused by the success of amusement parks. Rather than providing an escape from the urban spectacle, they offered a heightened version of it: speeding rides, repetitive noise, flashing electric lights, and transient crowds. But what many critics, then as now, failed to grasp is the possibility that these things might hold a powerful romantic allure of their own.

Visceral City

For Londoners 100 years ago, visiting an amusement park was a defining counterpart to life in the modern metropolis. By the turn of the 20th century, when the fast pace of crowds, travel, and urban life had become normal, observers noted that city-dwellers were growing desensitized. The idea that people living in cities develop a protective mental layer against the over-stimulation of modern life was formulated by the work of sociologist Georg Simmel (*The Metropolis and Mental Life*, 1903), and later by Sigmund Freud's notion of the "stimulus-shield."[14] These authors suggested that only extreme shocks could penetrate this protective psychological layer. Just as the amusement parks were becoming more popular, such shocks were increasingly deemed to be pleasurable.

Amusement park rides were thus stripped of all sensory buffers in order to reinject the sense of velocity and danger that had been diminished by upholstered, sealed railway carriages. The opportunity for interaction with strangers and physical intimacy on rides such as The Tickler, or in the quiet darkness of the River Caves, compensated for the indifference of the city street. The parks represented a unique space in which the stimulus-shield of modern life might be momentarily cast aside.

The search for intense experience—thrill-seeking—was (and is) understood as a defining characteristic of the modern psyche. In 1908, a journalist described his experience on the Scenic Railway as "a psychological revelation" in which "the modern man [...] enjoys primitive emotions in a scientific fashion."[15] The amusement parks provided an escape from the anonymity of urban life. In doing so, they catered for a shared desire for sensuous and immediate engagement with life, a desire that continues to drive urban pleasure-seeking trends. Today, even as techno-pleasures are taken for granted and as the 'shock' of the modern city has been internalized, urban crowds continue to be drawn to environments in which a purely emotional intensity might still be found.

[P]leisure

The postmodern blurring of lines between work and play has rendered distinctions between leisure and pleasure redundant. No longer fearful of pleasures of the senses, sex, food, and shopping permeate our public spaces and dominate our non-work lives. In such a context, it is perhaps not surprising to see thrilling kinesthetic pleasures making a comeback. Rather than seeking out immersive pleasurescapes, geographically separated from the everyday, we now find kinesthetic pleasures dotted around the city, inserted into familiar structures and enmeshed in the urban experience itself.

Epitomizing the current pleasure revival, Atelier Zündel Cristea, a French architectural studio, recently published plans for the rebirth of Battersea Power Station, another icon of London's skyline, as a museum of architecture, "a new site for architectural pleasures." Designed to encourage playfulness, the scheme weaves a giant curving scaffold in and around the heritage-listed building, creating a network of paths between the exhibition spaces. In an audacious twist, these aerial walkways in turn provide tracks for an enormous rollercoaster running on top.[16] The scheme pays homage to the hugely successful Festival of Britain Pleasure Gardens at Battersea in 1951. But it harks back even further, unwittingly perhaps, to an ambitious but unrealized Dream City project (complete with 200-foot electric tower and giant water chute) proposed in 1908, at the height of the Edwardian amusement park rush.[17]

1 "At the Franco-British Exhibition," *The Times* (June 9, 1908), 8.

2 Javier Pes, "Kiralfy, Imre (1845–1919)," *Oxford Dictionary of National Biography* (Oxford: Oxford University Press, 2004) [Online].

3 From the prospectus of Topsy Turvy Pleasure Railway Southend on Sea Ltd (April 17, 1903), The National Archive, BT 31/10260/77063.

4 Mary Banham & Bevis Hillier (eds), *Tonic to the Nation: The Festival of Britain, 1951* (London: Thames & Hudson, 1976), 121–124. Over 18 million people visited the amusement park after it passed to private ownership in 1954. "£1m improvement scheme for Battersea funfair," *The Times* (March 24, 1971), 3.

5 Richard Hoggart, *The Uses of Literacy: Aspects of Working Class Life with Special Reference to Publications and Entertainments* (Harmondsworth: Penguin, 1957), 205.

6 Erik Hedling, *Lindsay Anderson: Maverick Film-Maker* (London: Cassell, 1998).

7 "leisure, n.," and "pleasure, n.," Oxford English Dictionary Online (September 2014).

8 See Roy Porter's chapters "Enlightenment and Pleasure" and "Material Pleasures," in *Pleasure in the Eighteenth Century* (New York: NYU Press, 1996). Also see Jonathan Conlin (ed.), *The Pleasure Garden, From Vauxhall to Coney Island* (Philadelphia: University of Pennsylvania Press, 2012).

9 The popular cultures that evolved around the sensory pleasures of drinking and sex were the cause of particular alarm amongst Victorian reformers. See James Walvin, *Leisure and Society 1830-1950* (London: Longman Group Ltd, 1978), 33–46; Brad Beaven, *Leisure, Citizenship and Working Class Men in Britain, 1850-1945* (Manchester: Manchester University Press, 2005), 47.

10 Cited in Rojek, *Ways of Escape: Modern Transformations in Leisure and Travel* (Basingstoke and London: Macmillan Press, 1993), 17.

11 Ibid., 32–34.

12 Lauren Rabinovitz discusses new ideas about pleasure in the context of American exhibitions in "Urban Wonderlands: Siting Modernity in turn-of-the-century Amusement Parks," *European Contributions to American Studies* 45 (2001): 89.

13 I have borrowed this phrase from Cecilia Tichi, who uses it to describe the industrialized landscape of 19th-century America in *Shifting Gears: Technology, Literature, Culture in Modernist America* (London: University of North Carolina, 1987), xiii.

14 See David Frisby, *Fragments of Modernity:*

Pleasure-seeking Londoners will, unfortunately, have to look elsewhere for their next urban thrill fix. In 2012, the Power Station was bought by a Malaysian consortium developing the site into luxury residential, office, and retail space. Economic forces and the exponential rise of real estate value in London dictate that no developer would ever seriously contemplate a space dedicated entirely to fun. Instead it has become almost mandatory for landmark projects to weave a pleasure narrative into their sales pitch. At the Power Station, this is represented by the inclusion of a glass elevator transporting visitors to the top of a reconstructed chimney, from which two floors of apartments on the roofs of the turbine annexes can be surveyed.

Despite the trumpeting of each new novelty as bigger, more innovative, more exhilarating than the last, we remain timid in our pleasure-seeking. The real delight that the best architectural interventions have brought to the city is undeniable. But, held up to the otherworldly adventures pioneered by the Edwardian amusement parks, today's urban pleasures appear fragmented and fleeting.

Theories of Modernity in the Work of Simmel, Kracauer and Benjamin (Cambridge, MA: MIT Press, 1986), 73–4; James Strachey (ed.), *Sigmund Freud: Beyond the Pleasure Principle*, Vol. 4 (London: Hogarth Press & Institute of Psychoanalysis, 1974), 20–22.

15 "A Fortune in a Thrill," *The Sunday Chronicle* (Manchester) (August 23, 1908).

16 Atelier Zündel Cristea, http://www.zundelcristea.com/architecture/battersea-power-station (accessed December 8, 2014).

17 "The Dream City," *World's Fair* (March 14, 1908), 10.

Opposite:
Battersea Power Station scheme, London (Atelier Zündel Cristea, 2013)

STEFAN AL

THE EVOLVING ARCHITECTURE OF PLEASURE

Stefan Al is a Dutch architect, urban designer, and Associate Professor of Urban Design at the University of Pennsylvania. Al's research focuses on the evolution of urban form from a global perspective, with articles published in the *Handbook of Architectural Theory*, the *Berkeley Planning Journal*, *Urban China*, and elsewhere. He has edited the books *Factory Towns of South China* (2012) and *Villages in the City: A Guide to South China's Informal Settlements* (2014), and is currently writing a book on Las Vegas called *The Strip*.

+ HISTORY, URBAN DESIGN

The Las Vegas Strip is one of the few streets in the world that has radically reinvented itself multiple times in an effort to attract tourists to this isolated spot in Nevada's Mojave Desert. As competition between casinos has intensified over time, casino developers have collectively changed the Strip from its early incarnation as a desert oasis through to the high-design streetscape of today. This essay describes the various phases that Las Vegas has gone through and discusses the evolving American taste for pleasure that has acted as a catalyst for architectural change.

Desert Oasis (1940s to 1950s)

In 1941, Thomas Hull built El Rancho, the first casino resort on a stretch of the Los Angeles Highway that was to become the future Las Vegas Strip. At the time, it was nothing more than a dusty, potholed road stretching through the Mojave Desert, connecting Los Angeles to Las Vegas. Since most of the existing casinos were built downtown, locals were beyond surprise: "Two miles out! Middle of a desert! To promoters and builders in Vegas proper, the idea was insane."[1]

But downtown casinos, built on smaller parcels, did not have the space for pools or landscaping. On his more spacious Las Vegas Strip parcels, Hull built a "desert oasis," planting a lavish lawn immaculately maintained by a staff of 10 gardeners. He imported fully-grown trees and rock waterfalls, soaking up to 10 million gallons of water per month from Las Vegas' groundwater wells.[2] And he dug a pool, and made sure that everyone would notice it. *The Saturday Evening Post* wrote, "[i]nstead of hiding its glittering swimming pool in some patio, they stuck it in their show window, smack on Route 91. It was a stroke of showmanship. No traveler can miss the pool, few can resist it."[3]

Hull had started an important trend. By the 1950s, all casino complexes along the Las Vegas Strip relied on the desert oasis motif to attract passing drivers. The heightened contrast of lavish lawns and pools in the middle of the desert proved a captivating combination. It was so appealing that drivers heading to downtown would stop before they even got to the more-established downtown casinos. At the end of the 1950s, a dozen such desert oases lined the Las Vegas Strip, with barely any traces of the desert remaining. By 1962, the springs had stopped flowing and the green meadows that gave Las Vegas its name ("Las Vegas" is Spanish for "the meadows") had all but faded away.

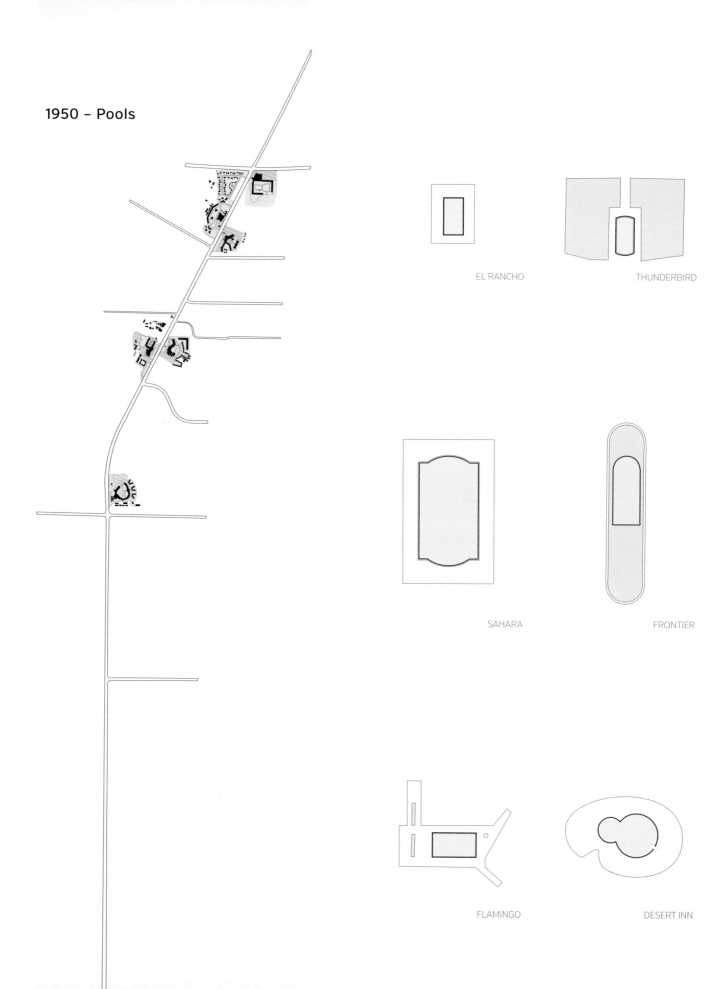

1950 – Pools

EL RANCHO

THUNDERBIRD

SAHARA

FRONTIER

FLAMINGO

DESERT INN

1968 – Signs

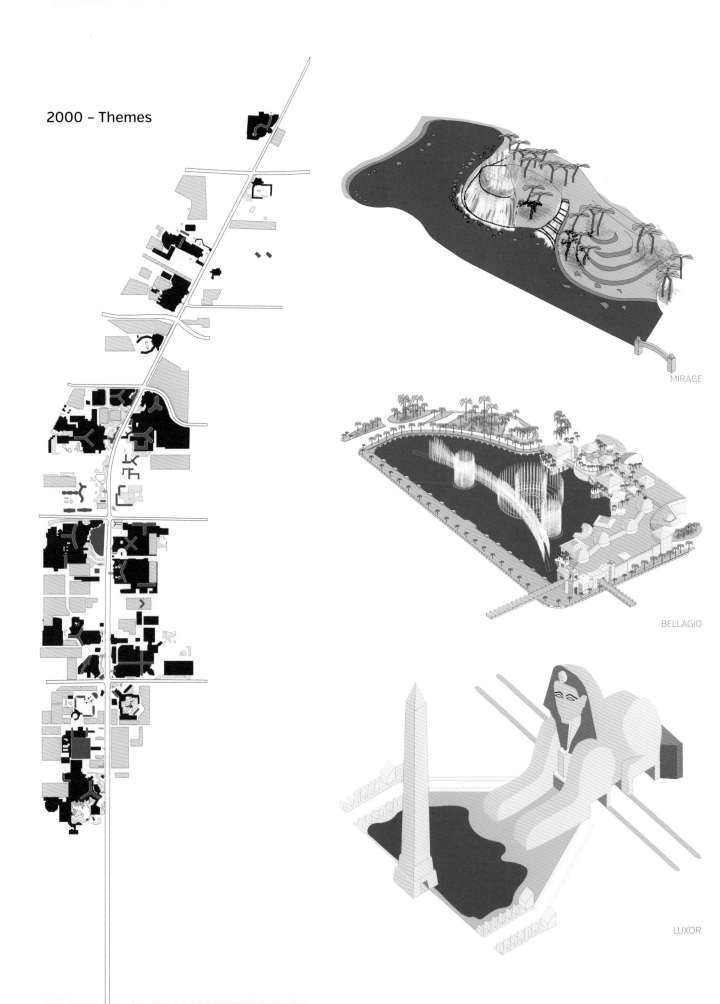

2000 – Themes

MIRAGE

BELLAGIO

LUXOR

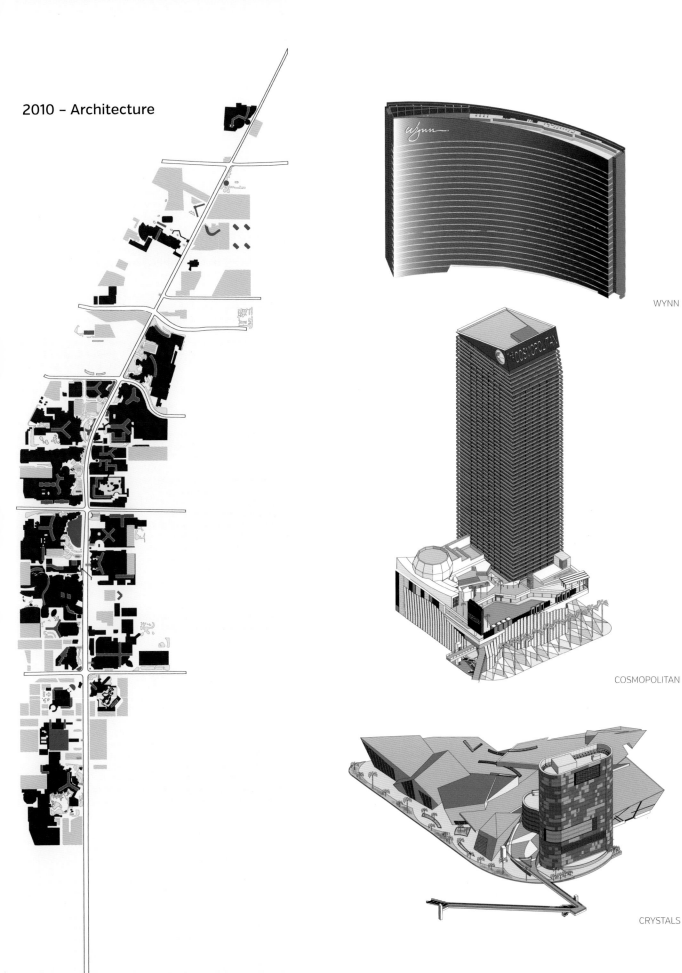

2010 – Architecture

WYNN

COSMOPOLITAN

CRYSTALS

A Forest of Signs (1960s to 1970s)

In 1955, Tony Cornero was building the Stardust, a 1,000-room casino resort. Instead of fussing with landscaping, he placed vast swaths of asphalt parking lots between the room wings, all of which were oriented to face the 16,500-square-foot casino, impossible to miss. But during a craps game at the Desert Inn, while his building was only 70% complete, Cornero collapsed against the craps table and died. "He had crapped out," a reporter wrote.[4]

John "The Barber" Factor, the black sheep half-brother of make-up magnate Max Factor, took over to finish the project, which had until then about as much personality as a warehouse. The Young Electro Sign Company (YESCO) was brought in. They covered the Stardust's generic casino and faceless hotel rooms with a sign the length of a jumbo jet, containing 7,100 feet of neon tubing and 11,000 light bulbs. It depicted a planetary system gravitating to a plastic globe. Beams of light radiated from the 'earth' into a sawtooth top, among flickering stars and plastic planets. On both sides of the earth was the word Stardust, its Electra-jag font filled with light bulbs – the 'S' alone contained 975 lamps.

The Stardust's efficiently laid-out rooms, cross-financed by the casino, helped mass-produce the Strip vacation, making it affordable to middle-class tourists who were charged only $6 a night. Putting up a prominent and glamorous front allowed for less-expensive architecture to exist at the back. While getting to the room wings might have been a sobering experience, entering the front of the casino was something special. The sign distracted from anonymous architecture and gave the middle class, despite their stay in a small box, a celestial experience away from the everyday.

As icing on the cake, YESCO placed a rocket, looking like an oversized firecracker, adjacent to the road. Tourists could be photographed with the rocket against the background of the intergalactic sign. It functioned as invaluable advertising for the casino. A reporter noted it was a "real traffic-stopper," "unique, unusual, and compelling," and that it "undoubtedly will prove to be the most photographed item in the area."[5]

The success of the Stardust saw the sign strategy escalate among the Strip casinos. Take, for instance, the flaming red Dunes sign, as tall as a 20-story building, or the electric Thunderbird façade, as long as two football fields. The Strip's identity became inextricably linked to the thousands of light bulbs and miles of neon – for in Las Vegas, neon was measured not by the foot, but by the mile.

As a result, Las Vegas in the 1960s and 1970s turned into a forest of neon signs. Tom Wolfe wrote, "Las Vegas is the only town in the world whose skyline is made up neither of buildings, like New York, nor trees, like Wilbraham, Massachusetts, but signs. One can look at Las Vegas from a mile away on Route 91 and see no buildings, no trees, only signs. But such signs! They tower. They revolve, they oscillate, they soar in shapes before which the existing vocabulary of art history is helpless."[6]

Disneyland (1980s to 1990s)

In 1989, Steve Wynn placed a lagoon and an eight-story volcano, spewing columns of smoke and flame, in front of the Strip's newest casino resort, the Mirage. Artificial scent masked the sulfuric gas emitted by the flames, and made the volcano smell like piña colada. The environment was further enhanced by the recorded sounds of chirping birds, giving way to roaring thunder every 15 minutes when the volcano 'erupted'. On its opening day, 200,000 people witnessed the first 'eruptions' of the volcano, twice as many as expected.[7]

Fueled by Wynn's success, Bill Bennett promptly built Excalibur, a 30-story castle where Merlin exchanged fireballs with a three-story dragon. Not to be outdone, the Mirage responded with a pirate village where skirmishing pirates set a British battleship on fire, then sank it, every hour. The Luxor soon followed with a hollow pyramid large enough to stack nine jumbo jets, with the world's brightest laser beam shooting from the top, fronted by a 10-story, laser-eyed Sphinx, upon which Kirk Kerkorian built an equally large cubist lion, its paws stretched out, its eyes staring down the Sphinx, with Dorothy, Scarecrow, and the Tin Man emerging from underneath its chin.

As outrageous as all this sounds, the 'Disneyfication' of the Strip was based on cold-blooded calculation. When the Disney Corporation had become the largest entertainment conglomerate in the world in the 1980s, casino developers mimicked Disney, hoping to attract their own share of the traveling family market. Wynn took the first plunge. When his volcano turned heads, others followed, and a true theme park war raged on the Strip. It led to a highly original era of Disney expressionism, and spawned companies specializing in fiberglass rock and pyrotechnics, building themed environments worldwide. The entire theme design industry's slogan had even become: "You don't look up 'volcano' in the Yellow Pages."[8]

By the end of this new phase of the Strip, Disney's Animal Kingdom had been imported too. With all the bottlenose dolphins, white tigers, and toucans flown into the Mojave Desert, just a familiar rodent was missing to complete the picture – if only its copyright had expired, the Strip would undoubtedly have added a mouse ear–shaped casino to its skyline.

But unlike the serenity of Disney's monopoly of Main Street, USA, multiple companies competed for the Las Vegas Strip. In the Strip's distortion of Disneyland, pharaohs, pirates, hawkers, protesters, and honking cars all vie for attention. For a little more than a decade, Las Vegas led the world in Disney expressionism. And best of all, unlike Disneyland, it was free.

High-Design Streetscape (2000s to 2010s)

In 2004, MGM Mirage Chairman Terry Lanni announced "a significant new direction for our city and our company."[9] The company planned to build a new casino resort with a "city-like ambiance." Project City Center was born.

But MGM Mirage did not plan a 'city' like the adjacent New York-New York, with its replica of the Manhattan skyline and Statue of Liberty. The company tapped deep into the pool of architectural talent to create an 'original' skyline, involving world-renowned architects Rafael Vinoly, Norman Foster, Cesar Pelli, and Daniel Libeskind. In contrast to the typical casino complex, Libeskind described his contribution as a "rich, urbane, cosmopolitan scheme, one you could find in New York or in Paris." His building connected to the sidewalk "the way buildings do in Manhattan," and let in natural light. He claimed his project with his trademark jagged shapes, attempting "to give a world of simulacra something original and real."[10]

Ehrenkrantz, Eckstut and Kuhn Architects, famous for designing Manhattan's Battery Park, were commissioned to design the master plan of the resort. Going against the tradition to shun gamblers from daylight, they designed a number of open spaces in the resort, including 'pocket parks' and boulevards. Here the majority of the company's 40-million-dollar 'public' art program was displayed, including sculptures by world-class artists Henry Moore, Claes Oldenburg, and Coosje Van Brugge.

In the new millennium, Las Vegas casino moguls vigorously embraced the 'Bilbao Effect:' the belief that a building designed by a star architect would attract visitors, like Frank Gehry's Guggenheim museum had revitalized Bilbao. In particular, they sought to attract a younger and wealthier demographic, since it turned out families did not bring in enough money. This new brand-centric demographic did not want Disneyland-style fakes. They wanted originals.

As the casino complex came to include avant-garde architecture, high-designed public spaces, and elite art, the sidewalks were upgraded as well. Since the Strip had become an increasingly dense pedestrian place, with only a few corporations controlling most of the land, they started to pay attention to the public realm, building terraces, benches, cobblestone walkways, and active street fronts. What was once a series of asphalt parking lots is in the process of becoming a "neighborhood environment," beginning with the MGM Mirage–commissioned park currently being designed by New York landscape architecture firm !melk.

After seven decades of development of the Las Vegas Strip, a site of extreme market-led urbanization, the biggest surprise is how casino corporations have become interested in implementing good planning and urban design principles. Despite its loose planning conditions, the Strip is finally evolving from a car-oriented highway to a pedestrian-oriented boulevard.

1 Katharine Best & Katharine Hillyer, *Las Vegas, Playtown U.S.A.* (New York: D. McKay Co., 1955), 61.

2 Pam Goertler, "The Las Vegas Strip: The Early Years," *Casino Chip and Token News* (Summer 2007).

3 Wesley Stout, "Nevada's New Reno," *Saturday Evening Post* (October 31, 1942).

4 Bob Holdorf, *Las Vegas Review-Journal* (July 31, 1955).

5 "Flashing Color Display Featured in Stardust Sign," *Las Vegas Review-Journal* (July 1, 1958).

6 Tom Wolfe, *The Kandy-Kolored Tangerine-Flake Streamline Baby* (New York: Bantam Books, 1977), 7.

7 Christina Binkley, *Winner Takes All: Steve Wynn, Kirk Kerkorian, Gary Loveman, and the Race to Own Las Vegas* (New York: Hyperion, 2008), 26.

8 Eben Shapiro, "All About/Theme Park Spinoffs Need a Little Fantasy? A Bevy of New Companies Can Help," *The New York Times* (March 10, 1991).

9 Associated Press, "MGM MIRAGE to Develop a Dramatic Urban Environment for the New Millennium," (November 11, 2004).

10 Justin Davidson, "The Liberation of Daniel Libeskind," *The New York Times* (September 30, 2007).

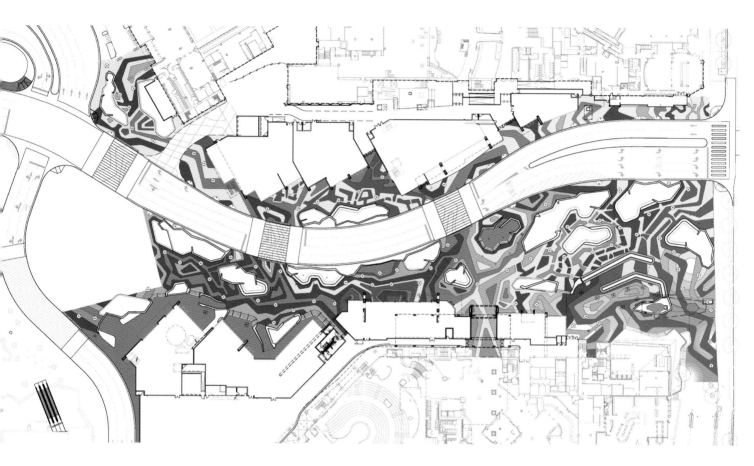

Jerry van Eyck is a landscape architect, industrial designer and former principal of West 8. His New York–based studio !melk is developing the first park and pedestrian promenade on the Las Vegas Strip. The project marks a significant change in the urban evolution of the city and will create, as Jerry puts it, a place that is "uniquely, authentically Las Vegas."

+ How do you feel about working in the Las Vegas desert, coming from a background of Polders in the Netherlands?

Since I was a young boy, I've always been fascinated by American Pop Culture, its iconography and depicted lifestyle, so ending up living here and working in Las Vegas almost seems like fate to me. I think that, looking back and analyzing this, you could say that I'm probably attracted to the desert because it is the exact opposite of the Netherlands. While my birth country is wet, regulated, and constrained, the Las Vegas region is dry, vast, and extremely powerful. I love the desert–all of them–the Sonoran, the Chihuahuan, and the Mojave Desert in which Las Vegas is situated...it's really fantastic stuff.

+ What is your favorite thing to do in Las Vegas?

Actually, it is to get on a Harley and get out of town and just ride!

+ So you don't like to gamble?

No, I don't gamble. Of course, I know that's what Las Vegas is known for, and when people think of Las Vegas they think of the Strip, but the Strip is basically the equivalent of Times Square here in New York. It's an entertainment district. The Strip is not Las Vegas. The stigma is that Las Vegas is crazy and over the top, but that's not the city itself, that's the Strip.

Above: The plan for the first park on the Strip

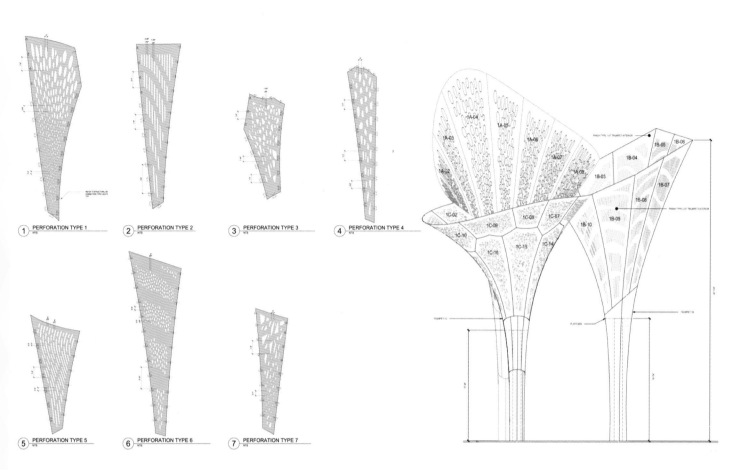

1 PERFORATION TYPE 1
NTS

2 PERFORATION TYPE 2
NTS

3 PERFORATION TYPE 3
NTS

4 PERFORATION TYPE 4
NTS

5 PERFORATION TYPE 5
NTS

6 PERFORATION TYPE 6
NTS

7 PERFORATION TYPE 7
NTS

Above: Shade structures for the park

+ How much did Koolhaas or Venturi and Scott Brown influence your attitude while working on the Strip?

Venturi and Scott Brown's books are some of the most influential books in architecture theory ever. But when we started this project, I realized that their analyses on Las Vegas, that were such a source of inspiration for me and many others in the profession, were basically outdated. They're not valid or applicable anymore: they're from another era.

We've learned so much more about Las Vegas by now, especially regarding the politics of it and the business side, and the ownership situation. The properties and hotels along the Strip used to be, you know, owned by "private entrepreneurs," who in general had home bases in Chicago. Have you seen Scorsese's "Casino"? That's how it was! A few decades later, the big corporations started taking over, all publically traded, all based with serious business models and boards. So Venturi and Scott Brown's analysis of the Strip of the 60s and 70s remained valid for a while, and their methods and techniques of course still are, but gradually, without anybody noticing, their Las Vegas changed. The original iconography that's still in people's memory of the place has disappeared and is being replaced by the constantly evolving business philosophies of the big corporations. Today, there are only a handful [of corporations] that control the Strip. And their decisions are always market-driven. People's expectation for going to Vegas and the things they like to do there have also changed. For example, people don't go there anymore to gamble; the entertainment industry in Vegas has become much more diversified, and because of that the owners will have to adjust their business strategies to be able to monetize from the latest trends and market demands. The main sources of income today are conventions, and the hotels themselves with their restaurants and clubs. But most importantly, the Strip itself has changed. Originally designed for cars, it's now turned into a pedestrian boulevard attracting 40 million visitors a year!

A view of the new boulevard and the future park and stadium

+ Is that why they are bringing in landscape architects now? Because of the shift away from vehicular traffic?

The traffic is still there, but in addition to that there are all these pedestrians that the casinos never imagined would walk miles and miles in the desert. It's only recently that property owners have realized this enormous shift. Our client, MGM Resorts International, owns about 65% of the properties on the Strip and for the first time in history it's in a position to be thinking about the Strip in a contiguous way – in terms of connectivity and cohesion let's say, instead of property by property, hotel by hotel, theme by theme. The themed hotels are still there, but they're seen as passé and sort of fading. It's the outdoor connectivity between the hotels that is getting the attention now.

+ So your current project on the Strip is a test case for converting the Strip from cars and kitsch to a more pedestrianized place. How's it working out?

It's working out well. I mean...it's a process. We're dealing with a situation where we're in the Wild West, right? We're in America. So the car is still very prominently present. But people understand that pedestrian infrastructure is definitely a force to be dealt with. Even more, it's a presence that the property owners realize they can make business from. So we're designing promenades, plazas, open spaces, and the first public park in the history of the Strip; but at the same time the architecture of the properties is being adapted. The building facades are opening up and the hotels are spilling out towards the street, with restaurants, shops, and sidewalk cafes. Property owners are investing in changing the functionality of the hotels, but they're also investing in public space, because that's where the people are. It's almost a revolution! They're investing in the "void" and not just in the real estate.

+ How do you reconcile landscape architecture's pastoral tendencies with the Vegas aesthetic?

I'm not sure what you mean by "pastoral tendencies," do you mean the trends of generic green fluffy stuff? Well our project, indeed, is not about that. It's funny, but we actually think that we are trying to come up with something that is uniquely, authentically, Las Vegas. Sounds really odd, right? Because there is basically no authenticity in Las Vegas: never has been except for, you know, being non-authentic. Nevertheless, we are actually actively grounding everything, blending everything, in a sort of unique context that is inspired by the history and geography of Las Vegas. Our park, for example, is reinstating what Las Vegas once was, before it became 'Vegas': a green oasis in the desert, with groves of trees, and springs, and water. Of course we'll mix it with today's reality of commerce. On top of that lies the philosophy of coherence and the contiguous Strip-wide design approach that makes our project different from any other in the past. It's a completely new situation.

+ Was that part of the client's thinking or something you brought to the table?

Oh, it definitely started on the level of MGM's senior management. I consider them as the visionaries behind the project and I can't help myself actually seeing them as New Urbanists even! We were just the lucky ones to shape a new philosophy. There is going to be this transition of the Las Vegas Strip becoming an actual urban entity and we're doing it! Change is happening! The first phase—right in front of the two hotels New York-New York and Monte Carlo—is well under way and we're breaking ground for the park. We're diluting the themes of the hotels quite a bit, and we're developing a middle-ground vocabulary that connects everything. Our project consists of coordinated materials, patterns, geometries, vegetation, microclimate, and functionality.

+ If the original iconography is going to be erased in the future, how do you see Vegas distinguishing itself?

Don't worry, Vegas will be Vegas for a while; but think about it, Haussmann built Paris with its typical Parisian boulevard structure, right? I think that nobody will disagree that those boulevards, including the Champs-Élysées, are quite iconic. Well, the Strip is to Vegas what the Champs-Élysées is to Paris! It will remain an entertainment district though, and be full of commerce, and be a tourist destination with its own unique history, but in terms of use perhaps, it'll grow more towards its Parisian counterpart. That's what's happening now. The hotels are losing the importance of themes: Las Vegas is not about cheap illusions anymore, or about families. Perhaps our design of the boulevard itself, with its vocabulary, materiality, and sustainability systems, could be the carrier of the future Las Vegas brand. I think that would be great.

+ Is there any symbolism in your Vegas work, and if so, where does it come from?

Hmm, the only symbolism I can think of is the fact that we're re-creating what Las Vegas once was, that got erased over time: a green and lush area, somewhere in the Mojave Desert. In the 1800s, travelers through the desert gravitated towards it, initially to feed their horses, later to tank water into their steam trains. After a very weird, 'glitterful' detour – we're arriving back to where it all began. We're doing this park in Las Vegas, and it's once again a green oasis, a refuge in the desert with shade and with water. And with trees, with actual desert trees, not with non-native palm trees! We're getting rid of the fake, and that's the main symbolism in our project.

+ How much was the idea of sustainability pushed for meaningful impact versus just a greenwash?

Very much so, but again, it's a process. Nevada is one of the states where water consumption is heavily subsidized, and it should not be! Water in New York State is more expensive than it is in Vegas! We're still integrating sustainable systems in our project. We're working on a method to make our park completely free of consumption of city water by using MGM's own water for everything: for irrigation as well as the water features. We are fortunate that our client wants to make a change and so do we. But it's a can of worms, since it's unheard of in Nevada. Our park is LEED Gold, but you know, LEED is also very arbitrary and capricious. If something is LEED certified, it doesn't mean it's sustainable in my opinion.

+ Could Vegas become a sustainable city, a walkable city? Or is this just a make-over for the Strip?

Las Vegas is a typical American sprawl city with a huge, over-dimensioned roadway system. There are only a few areas in Las Vegas—the downtown area and the Strip—where because of its density we have the opportunity to create something that resembles an urban fabric. So there, yes, but a few blocks to the west or east it's just very generic Americana.

It's pretty cool to be part of an historic shift but you know, there is such a stigma about Las Vegas. People ask us silly questions such as, "how is it to work in an environment where you can do anything you want?" Whoa, it's the opposite! To get anything done requires a lot of energy from us – constantly motivating people and showing proof of what needs to be achieved, can actually be done, or has been done before. We use our optimistic attitude to mobilize everyone, to let everybody believe in it. For the people involved, what we do is extremely unconventional. It's extremely alien and sometimes disturbing for them because we're stirring up conventions. But we're doing it anyway because we're able to show that we're right! If the success of public space design can be measured from an actual increased revenue, they're able to think twice. It's great to have the support of such a visionary and powerful client (MGM's senior management). Las Vegas is changing – for the better if you ask me. It's not going to happen overnight, but the process has been set in motion.

GIVE HER A DIAMOND THAT CAN BE SEEN FROM OUTER SPACE

A DIAMOND IS FOR PLEASURE

PLEASURE PIT

In Botswana, the world's most valuable diamond mine grows deeper every day. More than 1.5 billion dollars of diamonds are extracted from Jwaneng Mine each year, accounting for roughly 15% of the world's diamond production. In the process, a machine-made landscape has been created, in stark contrast to the flat terrain of the Kalahari Desert.

The open pit, from which the diamonds are unearthed, will eventually become 2,700 feet deep: half the depth of the Grand Canyon. The waste rock removed from the pit is piled up into large hills. The ore, which contains only 0.00005% diamond, is crushed up and filtered automatically by a series of x-rays, magnets, and lasers. The tailings then pass through more than three miles of conveyor belts before they are dumped to the south of the pit.

The Jwaneng Mine continues to expand, despite the fact that diamonds of a similar quality can now be produced in a laboratory for a fraction of the cost. Consumers are persuaded to pay a higher price for diamonds that are mined from the earth because they are led to believe the romantic notion that they are natural. In fact, the beauty of a diamond is only revealed after it has been mined, cut, and polished.

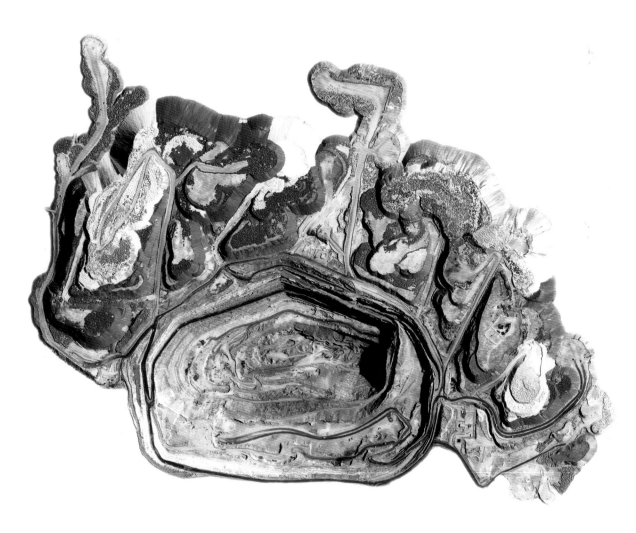

1 Mile

MAGDALENA SABAT
SPATIAL REGULATION OF THE SEX INDUSTRY IN NEW YORK CITY

Magdalena Sabat is a doctoral candidate with the Department of Media, Culture, and Communication at New York University, and an interdisciplinary researcher in the fields of visual and cultural studies and urbanism. She writes on urban gentrification, development, and the sex industry. Sabat holds a Master of Arts from the University of Amsterdam and currently works in research and communication at the Institute Without Boundaries in Toronto, Canada.

✛ URBAN STUDIES, SOCIOLOGY, CULTURAL STUDIES

A New York Dolls ad swishes by on top of a taxi on 2nd Avenue. The smiling blonde is a regular and recognizable feature of the streetscape to any New Yorker. The New York Dolls Gentleman's Club has been in operation since the early 1990s; it is one of the city's longest-running and most widely known strip clubs.[1] New York Dolls has remained in place, even as the rest of the city has undergone dramatic gentrification.

During the late 1980s and throughout the 1990s, New York's municipal governments sought to drive out the sex industry from the city center and transform the city into a clean, safe, and economically prosperous place. Through legal and spatial strategies, both the Giuliani and the Bloomberg administrations zoned out pornography and placed strict limits on adult businesses. The cleanup of Times Square, which was historically a major red light district, is seen as the pinnacle achievement of these policies and emblematic of the transformation of the city.[2] By the end of the 1990s, the municipality's actions had dramatically altered the presence of the sex industry in New York and set a future framework for how adult entertainment could exist in the city. But these policies did not eradicate sex business; rather, they contributed to its displacement and in some ways encouraged new forms of the sex trade that were emerging in parallel with the development of the Internet.[3]

Globally, the sex industry is estimated to produce billions in profits, but the actual size of the sector and the profits generated by it are unknown. What is apparent, however, is that the sector has become highly globalized, organized, competitive, and diverse, and that it is increasingly tied to mass consumerism, leisure, and tourism.[4] New organizational structures and commercial practices in the sex trade point to changes in its urban geographical distribution. Specifically, research is suggesting that the sector is no longer primarily tied to the marginal spaces of cities.[5] Instead the sex industry can be present in various ways—both grounded and virtual—throughout a city's landscape.[6]

In light of the diversification of sex industry practices, and research that suggests these practices are embedded in the formal leisure and tourist economies, it is more appropriate to think of New York's sex industry like that taxi driving on 2nd Avenue – a consistent and embedded part of urban life instead of something in opposition to it. What is needed are new ways of thinking about the sex industry and its spatial regulation in cities.

Regulating Sex Vice in New York City

The sex industry has a complicated urban geography because it exists in visible, invisible, and ephemeral ways. Yet this diversity has traditionally not been acknowledged by law enforcement and the public. Historically, the visible parts of the sex sector have been the focus of public attention, leading to problematic regulation and a misunderstanding of the parameters of the sector. Targeting visible sex vice has been a way to demonstrate the control of public morality and the 'deviant other,' as well as separating 'moral' and 'immoral' parts of society.[7] Thus, the urban geography of the sex industry and how visible it is (and in what ways) varies from place to place in parallel with established moral standards.

In the United States, legal sex industry businesses operate under the umbrella of adult entertainment. These businesses cannot include prostitution,[8] but can be highly suggestive of it, as in the case of the escort and massage advertisements found in the back of most mainstream newspapers and magazines. Generally, adult entertainment is legal providing it respects public laws on indecency and obscenity and does not cause a neighborhood disturbance.[9] This means that the way the sex industry makes itself visible in cities is highly spatial. It relates to how the sector appears on the street and what relationship the business has with its neighbors.

The cleanup of Times Square exemplifies traditional attitudes, policies, and actions towards the public visibility of the sex industry. In the 1990s, Mayor Rudolph Giuliani launched his

famous 'Quality of Life Campaign' against criminality in New York City. He was a vehement opponent of adult entertainment and pushed to eliminate visible pornography from the city's landscape by instituting anti-pornography zoning laws. The main zoning law, passed in 1995, prohibited adult establishments within 500 feet of one another, as well as within 500 feet of a school, church, or residential area.[10] He also created special zones where adult businesses were permitted. Given the density and mixed-use character of most of New York's inner-city neighborhoods, the visibility of adult business was severely curtailed in Times Square and the rest of Manhattan. Many adult businesses were pushed out from the center and others fought battles in court to remain open.[11]

In addition to new urban planning restrictions, there was an emphasis on greater policing. Law enforcement officials practiced 'broken window' style policing, which encourages police officers to heavily target minor crimes in the belief that it will have a domino effect and prevent more-serious crimes.[12] One of the other legal measures both the Giuliani and the later Bloomberg administration used to control sex business in the city was the outdated Cabaret Law, which was enacted during Prohibition to ban dancing in nightclubs and bars without a cabaret license.[13] The use of this law in the 1990s is significant because it continues to be active and affects the operations of most bars in the city. In fact, 'spontaneous dancing' in bars without special permits is still illegal, meaning that the authorities have a greater control of all night entertainment.

Many books have been written on the transformation of Times Square, illustrating its past peep shows, movie houses, street corner hustlers, and prostitutes as an edgy and grimy urban environment that typified the New York City of the early 20th century. Little of that past is evident now. Times Square was restructured into a mainstream commercial real estate zone with shopping and tourist activities, representing for many the commercialization and privatization of public places.

Giuliani's policies used the discourse of 'secondary impacts' and 'community character' to effectively curtail the visibility of the sex economy and gentrify neighborhoods that were sought after for commercial city development,[14] but they are not the sole factor in the transformation of the sex economy in Times Square nor the other greatly changed sex margins in the city. Alexandra Murphy and Sudhir Venkatesh claim that many prostitutes moved their trade indoors.[15] Prostitutes who had once solicited directly in streets or bars began to more actively advertise sexual services over the Internet and in print media, and increasingly conducted their work in their homes as well as in hotels

- ● ADULT ENTERTAINMENT
- ◕ BURLESQUE THEATER
- ◔ GAY SAUNA
- ◕ STRIP CLUB
- ◔ MASSAGE PARLOR
- ◕ HISTORICALLY SIGNIFICANT

1 I do not promote or endorse New York Dolls or any other business mentioned herein.

2 The literature on Times Square is abundant. Two studies that stand out are Samuel Delany, *Times Square Red, Times Square Blue* (New York: NYU Press, 1999) and Marshall Berman, *Out on the Town: One Hundred Years of Spectacle in Times Square* (London: Verso, 2nd Edition, 2009).

3 See Alexandra K. Murphy & Sudhir Alladi Venkatesh, "Vice Careers: The Changing Contours of Sex Work in New York City," *Qualitative Sociology* 29 (2006): 129–54.

4 There are many studies looking at the changes in the sex industry. Barbara G. Brent, Crystal A. Jackson, and Kathryn Hausbeck have written extensively on the sex industry in connection with leisure and tourism, see *The State of Sex: Tourism, Sex and Sin in the New American Heartland* (New York: Routledge, 2009).

5 For instance, Sudhir Venkatesh argues New York City's illicit economies are omnipresent and challenge conventional social boundaries and spatial-geographical division: *Floating City* (New York: Penguin Books, 2014).

6 Ibid.

7 On this topic, I value the work of Phil Hubbard and Teela Sanders, who use the term 'moral geography' to describe a social drive to isolate and divide the people and practices deemed to be 'immoral' from the 'moral' or central parts of society: "Making Space for Sex Work: Female Street Prostitution and the Production of Urban Space," *International Journal* 27, no. 1 (2003): 75–89.

8 Prostitution in the United States is illegal, except in some counties of the state of Nevada, where there are openly legal brothels. Its visibility and organization varies greatly from place to place and relates to the attitude of local law enforcement and the public.

9 The terms indecency and obscenity are widely contested but very important to the public visibility of pornography and adult entertainment. Both relate to the notion of public material that is offensive to or culpable against 'communal' or prevalent moral standards.

10 The New York State Office of the General Counsel Andrew M. Cuomo outlines the New York City regulation of adult uses: http://www.dos.ny.gov/cnsl/lu03.htm.

11 Jim Yardley captures the mood of Giuliani's policy changes in "Sex Shops on the Defensive, But Far From Stamped Out," *The New York Times* (26 January 1999).

12 Broken window style policing has been criticized for disproportionately targeting people who are already vulnerable (and in some cases formally condoning greater police force) while at the same time failing to address the systematic social issues underlying petty crimes.

and brothels. For Murphy and Venkatesh, Giuliani's policies contributed to the growth of an indoor sex trade and added to a new "professional and careerist" approach by prostitutes.[16]

In particular, the aggressive targeting of the lower-end spectrum of the sex industry and homelessness throughout the central parts of the city in part dislocated street prostitution and the grittier clusters of the sex industry to the city's more peripheral areas.[17] A simple online map search of the city's strip clubs shows many sex industry businesses are intensified in less-affluent neighborhoods of Queens and Brooklyn. New York's largest concentration of street prostitution is today located in Hunts Point, an area of the South Bronx and one of New York's poorest neighborhoods. Hunts Point is commonly identified as New York's red light district, reflecting the common belief that the highest concentrations of the sex industry are found in poor urban neighborhoods, but these types of areas reflect only the most vulnerable people working in the sex sector, excluding workers of the industry that are more intertwined in the entertainment and leisure industries. The seeming 'blind eye policy' towards openly practiced street prostitution and the lack of investment in Hunts Point reiterates the argument that the municipal fight against the sex industry in New York City was primarily a struggle over the city's central spaces sought after for commercial development.

But even with the new laws and the influence of new technology on the sex sector, adult business remains strong in Manhattan. In Midtown, a primary focus of Giuliani's eradication policies, adult businesses continue to thrive, particularly in the commercial and tourist areas close to transport hubs such as the Port Authority bus terminal on 42nd Street and the entrance to the Lincoln Tunnel (which provides access to the suburbs).[18] The further commercialization of these areas, in preference to an increase in residential use, has allowed sex industry businesses that are tied to entertainment settings (like strip clubs) to become well established.

A Shifting Urbanism

It is difficult to imagine today's Time Square as a red light district, yet it was a marginal urban space for a large part of its history. There are many other pertinent reasons why, historically, municipal governments have limited the visibility of sex in the streets: I have only touched on the debates here. New York's gentrification shows a shift in urbanism that promotes the transformation of central urban margins into commercial and themed entertainment settings in order to increase tourism potential and the aesthetic value of the landscape of the city itself.[19] This trend has been connected to a global competition between major cities of the world for investment and tourism dollars. In the process, critics point out that like the transformation of Times Square, this kind of urbanism is turning our cities into inauthentic commercial simulations of social life, rather than thriving spaces for the communal negotiation of change.[20]

A recent, poignant example of this trend is the urban regeneration plan of the center of Amsterdam that has shut down over 40% of red light windows in the famous Red Light District of De Wallen. Similar to the 'secondary impacts' and 'community character' rhetoric employed to regenerate Times Square, the Dutch municipality argues the redevelopment of the district is a necessary step to counter human trafficking and reclaim public space for the citizens of Amsterdam. However, the plan's preferential treatment of large retailers and studies that suggest closing the district makes prostitutes more vulnerable to trafficking rather than safer from it argue that the transformation of the Amsterdam Red Light District is primarily about commercializing and privatizing central public space and not giving it back to the people.[21]

Although Amsterdam and New York are very different cities, with very different policies regarding the sex trade, these examples highlight that spatial eradication strategies often misunderstand the composition and relationship of the sex industry to the city, in addition to further marginalizing vulnerable populations. They also vividly show an aggressive privatization and commercialization of city space under the guise of promoting urban growth and prosperity.[22]

The geography and practices of the sex industry in New York City are extremely wide. The practitioners and users of these economies operate visibly, invisibly, and in ephemeral ways, in urban and suburban, private and public venues. Yet somehow the sex industry tends to be reduced to trafficking practices and imagined as threatening to the city's well-being. It is important to understand the sex industry as an embedded and moving part of the whole landscape of the city and, in that way, also a part of the regular life of its citizens. Yes, part of your life and mine. Every video, strip club, and pole dancing class, just like every brothel, is driven primarily by mainstream social desire and not by marginal players. Whatever our moral stance, the fact is that the sex industry is a part of the fabric of our cities. Urban regulation of the sex industry needs to better negotiate between the needs of the industry and public moral standards.

13 Historians claim the law was aimed at restricting the interracial mixing happening in dance clubs, particularly in the speakeasies in Harlem. The law was widely used to curb 'cabarets' and other dancing venues, where there could be an increased chance of drinking and adult business. See Adam Janos, "For Nightclubs, Life is No Cabaret Without a License," *The Wall Street Journal* [29 September 2014].

14 Marilyn Adler Papayanis, "Sex and the Revanchist City: Zoning out pornography in New York," *Environment and Planning D: Society and Space* 18, no. 3 [2000]: 341–53.

15 Murphy & Venkatesh, "Vice Careers."

16 Ibid.

17 It is important to note the work of Neil Smith on gentrification of New York City. In *The New Urban Frontier: Gentrification and the Revanchist City* [New York: Routledge, 1996], Smith illustrates vividly the violent struggle against gentrification and the systematic police violence that pushed lower-class segments of the city's population from the center.

18 The city also has many publically invisible but permanent sex industry establishments. Sex and swingers clubs, brothels, dungeons, independent prostitutes, and many other types of venues that operate away from the public eye can be found throughout the city. These types of venues tend to keep low visibility to avoid law enforcement. At the same time, it is common knowledge that local law enforcement often knows about prostitution venues in its jurisdiction and either practices 'blind eye' or 'unofficial regulation' of these types of places.

19 From the theoretical writing on this topic, notable is the term 'fantasy city,' used to describe this process by John Hannigan, *Fantasy City: Pleasure and Profit in the Postmodern Metropolis* [New York: Routledge, 1998].

20 For instance, see Sharon Zukin, *Naked City: The Death and Life of Authentic Urban Places* [Oxford: Oxford University Press, 2010] and Michael Sorkin [ed.], *Variations on a Theme Park: The New American City and the End of Public Space* [New York City: Hill and Wang, 1992].

21 Manuel B. Aalbers & Magdalena Sabat, "Re-making a Landscape of Prostitution: The Amsterdam Red Light District," *City* 16, no. 1–2 [2012]: 112–28.

22 Ibid.

Acknowledgements
In this short glance at gentrification and the sex industry in New York City I am indebted to many excellent studies, some of which I have mentioned here. Many thanks to the editorial team, in particular Tatum Hands. Thanks also to photographer Leanne Staples for use of her image "New York Dolls."

Opposite: 42nd Street, New York City, 1982

M ajor new public spaces in New York are designed for pleasure. Over the last 12 years, the City of New York has invested in the creation of photogenic playgrounds for adults and kids as instruments of economic and cultural stimulus. As New York learned from London's earlier public space renaissance (beginning with the transformation of the Thames South Bank in the 1990s, through construction for the 2012 Olympic Games), making life interesting for young people is good for business and pride of place.

New York's density and diversity argue for public outdoor recreation as a form of necessary infrastructure for health, sanity, and for the formation of community ties for newcomers. Though there is no shortage of places dedicated to pleasure in New York, outdoor public spaces offer free of charge the potential for physical, sensory pleasure in an increasingly mediated culture. Four of New York City's new parks create a window on current attitudes toward leisure as a public good, and the capacity of skilled landscape architects to conjure diverse pleasures.

East River Waterfront Esplanade

Ken Smith's East River Waterfront Esplanade ("the Esplanade") seeks to create a continuous edge uniting the destinations of Chinatown and the Seaport district, ferry landings, and helipads along a previously neglected, slim, two-mile stretch of waterfront from Lower Manhattan to East River Park, north of the Manhattan Bridge. It tucks a series of convivial spaces under the roof of the elevated highway, including an immensely popular outdoor gym, basketball half-courts, a cycling and walking path, sitting areas, and a dog run. Beyond the shadow of the highway, lush plantings, a lawn atop the ferry terminal, and waterside seating animate the edge.

Like all projects designed during Amanda Burden's tenure at the Department of City Planning, the Esplanade offers plentiful and diverse social seating. (The former Commissioner strongly believes that New Yorkers' enjoyment of public space rests on our sense of social comfort and personal space vis-à-vis the strangers and friends with whom we share the experience.) The Esplanade's most unusual seating configuration is a set of high stools at the bulkhead railing, widely spaced as if for solitary barflies meditating on the river (or as is more often the case, hunched over laptops and phones – an unintended tableau of people who don't know how to have fun).

Ellen Neises teaches landscape design at the University of Pennsylvania and directs RANGE, a landscape and policy practice that works on large-scale and large-scope problems involving land, water and development. Ellen co-led the PennDesign/OLIN team's work on a winning entry in the 2014 Rebuild by Design competition. As associate partner at James Corner Field Operations until 2010, she worked on Freshkills and other projects, but not the High Line.

ELLEN NEISES

PLEASURE CRAFT

The most physically arresting element of the Esplanade creates a means for us to appreciate the qualities of the rocky intertidal zone that characterized a good portion of primordial New York. Ken Smith Landscape Architecture's bold and beautiful use of materials–incorporating huge precast chunks of surface-scored concrete– produces a dynamic play of unexpected geometry, scale, texture, and marine process, as well as a worthy experiment in the design of contemporary maritime edges. This is the piece of the design that most carries the spirit and energy of the East River waterfront's past and also some melancholy as its transformation from work to leisure approaches completion.

The fourth phase of the Esplanade project, now under construction, will complete a new precinct of housing, play, historical venues (a number of them floating), and shopping on the former South Street Seaport site. Hoarding around the site invokes past uses and pleasures soon to be replaced by new, like this 1952 quote from Joseph Mitchell: "Every now and then, seeking to rid my thoughts of death and doom, I get up early and go down to the Fulton Fish Market. I usually arrive around five-thirty and take a walk through the two huge open fronted market sheds...the smoky riverbank smell, the racket the fishmongers make, the seaweedy smell, and the sight of this plentifulness, always give me a feeling of well being, and sometimes they elate me." The engagement of all the senses by the working maritime landscape that Mitchell describes is hard to approximate in an amenity-driven park.

Brooklyn Bridge Park

On the opposite side of the East River sits Brooklyn Bridge Park by Michael Van Valkenburgh Associates (MVVA). Brooklyn Bridge Park is a 65-acre pleasure ground in a vibrant, diverse, changing borough of 2.6 million people. The programming and design reflect back to us the dominant character and contradictions of the new Brooklyn.

The large former working piers on the site lent themselves to intensive programming. MVVA responded to the physicality of the piers and huge industrial sheds with brawny rigging, fixtures and material choices, super-scaled rip-rap, a rough and real harbor beach, and unfussy planting that features few individual specimens. The aesthetic, especially along the waterfront edge, is of a fresh, landscape-architectural "machine for living."

The politics were much tougher than the site. Even in liberal Brooklyn, some vocal, moneyed neighbors were concerned about the huge influx of young people of color who would come to use the waterfront park, and they slowed the build-out for years. A recent move by the new mayor to introduce affordable housing in the park district renewed tensions, and reminded us just how unpleasant pleasure can be.

Nicolai Ouroussoff, the New York Times architecture critic, wrote that he worried initially that "[t]he high number of playing fields, canoes and kayaks called for in the plan seemed to reflect a body-obsessed culture in a constant search for distractions. The social space imagined in Olmsted's radical vision [of the democratizing power of public space] was being reduced to a public workout area."[1] What I see at Brooklyn Bridge Park is play and sport, not exercise; friends, team-mates, and strangers in pick-up games sociably playing beach volleyball, basketball, soccer, and handball; skating, dancing, climbing, and swinging in the breeze off the water.

MVVA's design concentrates many different sport and play facilities with different demographics back to back, along a single tightly packed strip. The circulation design also creates close encounters with non-sporting visitors. Exactly what some residents feared did happen–the park attracts large numbers of young people from all over the borough and beyond–and it turns out to be wonderful.

Designing for universal pleasure, Marc Treib writes, is the best way to create meaning through landscape in a society of many identities. Pleasure strengthens attachment to places, and as shared pleasurable experiences accrue, a landscape gains shared cultural significance and meaning for diverse publics.[2] Robert Somol offers another take on designing for diverse publics that I think applies to Brooklyn Bridge Park. He says that the challenge for design politics today is to "project a credible vision of the collective," channeling differences that already operate "toward unforeseen ends...venturing forms and systems of organization that invite a new collective to coalesce."[3] Because it convenes and encourages even the reluctant to enjoy the diversity of the city, Brooklyn Bridge Park creates optimism about the collective – a needed revision of Olmsted's mission to civilize.

Governors Island

The main challenge to widespread enjoyment of Governors Island is the trek it takes to get there. Once there, the setting is unparalleled – you are effectively on the prow of a large ship in the center of the harbor. But as Nick Paumgarten wrote in *The New Yorker*, due to its location, Governors Island is afflicted with "useless beauty" and a low budget.[4] The island's planning and operations director, Leslie Koch, comes from a marketing background at Microsoft and thinks in terms of customer desire, competition among pleasure venues, and "killer apps" for a park that she says has to deliver "two and a half hours of delight" in order to attract return journeys, love, and capital.[5]

Several activities have defined the early-stage experience out there: bike rentals in a place without cars, art events, miniature golf, and hammock napping (an idea that grew from author Maira Kalman's suggestion that Governors "should be the island of a thousand hammocks"). Leslie Koch made all of these activities available before West 8 and Mathews Nielsen Landscape Architecture started to build, but the experience is being much enhanced by design. The planned creation of steep, craggy hillsides and canyons where there is now a flat plain is intended to control and dramatize the views and spatial experiences – a strategy of the picturesque. The forms and organization of the supporting formal gardens, plazas, pavilions, allées, hammock groves, and pathways are inspired by a variety of European landscape tropes recombined and updated.

The most compelling moment of the 2007 design competition that led to the selection of the West 8 team was when Adrian Geuze rode into the public meeting on a custom-design wooden bike, smiling ear to ear. He showed a concept slide with a Keith Haring–style cartoon of broccoli over a photograph of Governors Island and the built-out southern tip of Manhattan and said his island would be "as green as broccoli." Nothing else he showed mattered. Everyone there was picturing themselves as blithe, colorful Dutchmen on gorgeous bikes in a verdant place. Of all the elements of the West 8–led proposal, the wooden bikes were what stirred passions we didn't yet know we had. Owned by no one, and designed by landscape architects to ply their willfully invented grounds, the fleet of wooden bicycles cast freedom from inhibition as a project of the imagination.

It is interesting that in its second-place entry in the Governors Island design competition, James Corner Field Operations (JCFO) proposed a contrasting set of pleasures and experiences. JCFO trained its attention on exposure to the elements: cold, ice, wind, and waves. The ramparts were cut back to admit and engage the sea in a series of sublime hydraulic theatres – a strange sort of weather station that accentuated extremity rather than simply measuring it. Comforts were offered in the design, but they were paired with challenges and the intensity of 'roughing it.'

The appeal of the JCFO response to the site was the enlargement of experience in an *other world* of atmospheres, pastimes, sensations, and encounters unknown in the city. Under the alternate plan, the island was to be a means of communion with, and investigation of, the wild sea. And had it been built, we might have found such a place very useful as a catalyst to thought and public discussion about adaptation to rising seas and climate change, as well as a complement to the offerings of other leisure venues.

High Line

The High Line created a kind of park that was new to New York: the promenade to nowhere. In 2004, when the JCFO/Diller Scofidio + Renfro team proposed a design concept that accommodated a large public, many people were incredulous that anyone would bother to climb up to a narrow, elevated linear park built on a land-locked former freight rail structure, particularly with all that Hudson River Park (master planned by Mathews Nielsen) offered just a couple of blocks west.

Designers and urbanists have since written at length about *looking* as the chief program offered at the High Line. It was a technical design feat on the part of JCFO to make the cramped, 30-foot-wide space generous and open to all kinds of unexpected uses. In retrospect, it makes perfect sense that looking and being looked at in an intimately scaled set would inspire joyful exhibitionism and theatre. On that backdrop, everything people do looks good and photographs even better.

Most unexpectedly, the High Line turned plants into mass-market entertainment. While it is relatively easy to please the untrained eye with florid displays, it is much more difficult to offer a rich, repeatable, complex experience that engages both horticultural novice and expert. JCFO used the long line of the 1.6-mile project to gradually shift the plant palette from Piet Oudolf's ideal of an intricately variegated garden that draws its energy from controlled choreography of species lifecycles and forms at the south end to James Corner's original concept of large, wild masses of pioneer species at the north end. Sweeping from south to north–from urbane to spare and seemingly uncultivated–you walk an invented transect that delivers a unique botanical experience.

The story of the High Line and its many catalytic effects are emblems of New York's capacity for change and concentration of energy. For some, it reads as relentlessness of redevelopment and gentrification, but even they see its brighter notes. On opening day, everyone from neighborhood school kids to the mayor was wearing a button that read "I built the High Line," and they had. For insiders accustomed to battling to build public space, it was heartening to know that our profession, allied with the public, had the capacity to open up bureaucracy to risk. And in cities around the United States and abroad, the High Line invigorated people's sense of possibility of a potent role for landscape architecture in urban transformation.

Landscape As A Medium Of Pleasure

The four new signature parks discussed here offer diverse and substantial pleasures that complement New York City's 28,000+ other acres of public social landscapes and wilds. Parks geared for delivery of "two and a half hours of delight" do not lend themselves to extended family barbecues and birthday parties – the stock-in-trade for Inwood Hill Park, Flushing Meadows Corona Park, Barretto Point Park, Prospect Park, and hundreds of other New York City parks where we wheel in all the food, blankets, balls, and kites we need for a day with friends.

Due to the high density of programming, the new parks are also less amenable to unpackaged experiences, to contemplation and long talks. They do not have room to support big ecologies with substantial productive output. In other words, high-energy pleasure parks like the four discussed here cannot, and do not aim to, replace the city's "slow landscapes" – a term akin to "slow food," coined by Elizabeth Meyer to describe landscapes that do not deliver quick gratification or profits.[6]

Having ushered in fresh pleasures, these parks point to the potential for still-greater diversity of program in the future – challenging places that offer stimuli to thought, sensory experience, and greater engagement of the real New York. Contemporary parks often over-privilege visual and endorphin-inducing pleasures, reducing our exercise of other capacities. The sublimity, demanding nature, and 'prompt to thought' of the JCFO proposal for Governors Island suggest types of urban environments that introduce a wider range of stimuli, expanding our repertoire of behaviors, experience with environmental forces, and evolutionary fitness (or at least root us in our physical natures).

The engagement of all our sensibilities by the smells, energies, deep pleasures, and provocations of the working maritime landscape that Mitchell described at the Seaport points away from amenity parks to designs that interweave the real and the recreational, creating mixed precincts that feature and advance the function of the working city and urban fabrics. The next wave of park development in New York City, driven by climate and economic imperatives and resiliency design, will hopefully result in distinctive built works of infrastructure that support major ecology and industry, as well as pleasure.[7]

This approach would go far to address the buzz-kill critique of contemporary urban design, landscape, and architecture, roughly as follows:

> Strictly speaking, spatial design today is for the most part a-critically in the service of the primary task thrown up by the new phase of modernization and globalization: accommodating and giving shape to a leisured affluent society. The dozens of stylistically homogenous, photo-shopped collages aimed at seducing clients and 'housing consumers' abound with people devoting themselves to a *dolce far niente* [delightful idleness] in a world that appears to consist of nothing but entertainment and consumption.[8]

In total, if not each project individually, contemporary urban landscapes should project a less optimistic view of the world. Small-scale 'green' works that treat a little bit of water, create a tiny patch of habitat, or grow a *de minimus* amount of food create a false sense of ecological wellbeing, and suggest we are learning to live lightly on the land. If, as landscape architects, we are anxious about impending ecological change, we should take care not to let pleasure suppress and pacify. (What's that old joke about the arrangement of social seating on the Titanic?)

Pleasure and consciousness need not conflict. The richness of our medium, over others, is that designed landscapes are the means and the grounds where, for millennia, humans have struggled with existential questions and with the art of settlement. John Dixon Hunt tells us that gardens have always been a "focus of human speculations, propositions and negotiations concerning what it is to live in the world" – a means of coming to terms with our place in nature and time, all the while enjoying its many pleasures.[9]

Aerial View of Manhattan © Google. Map data © Landsat, 2014.

1 Nicolai Ouroussoff, "The Greening of the Waterfront," *The New York Times* (April 1, 2010).

2 Marc Treib, "Must Landscapes Mean," in Simon Swaffield [ed.] *Theory in Landscape Architecture: A Reader* (Philadelphia: University of Pennsylvania Press, 2002), 89–101.

3 Robert Somol, "Yes is More," in Roger Sherman [ed.] *LA Under the Influence: The Hidden Logic of Urban Property* (Minneapolis: University of Minnesota Press, 2010).

4 Nick Paumgarten, "Useless Beauty: What is to be done with Governors Island?" *The New Yorker* (August 31, 2009).

5 Ibid.

6 Elizabeth Meyer, "Slow Landscape. A New Erotics of Sustainability," *Harvard Design Magazine* 31 (2010). Freshkills Park is an example of such a process landscape in New York.

7 For example, PennDesign/OLIN's winning entry in the Rebuild by Design competition proposes a park in Hunt's Point, New York, that both protects the area from flooding and strengthens the operations of the local fish, meat, and produce markets.

8 Hans Ibelings, "Hedonistic Landscapes," in H. Ibelings [ed.] *Artificial Landscape: Contemporary Architecture, Urbanism* (Rotterdam: NAi Publishers, 2000), 172. Critique quoted is focused on contemporary projects in the Netherlands.

9 John Dixon Hunt, *A World of Gardens* (Chicago: University of Chicago Press, 2012), 6.

PHOEBE LICKWAR + THOMAS OLES

WHY SO SERIOUS, LANDSCAPE ARCHITECT?

Phoebe Lickwar is Assistant Professor of Landscape Architecture at the University of Arkansas' Fay Jones School of Architecture. She studied landscape architecture, art history, and education at Rhode Island School of Design and Harvard University, and practiced as an associate at PWP Landscape Architecture. Her writing and photography has been featured in the *Journal of Landscape Architecture* and juried exhibitions nationally.

Thomas Oles is Lecturer in Landscape Architecture at the Edinburgh College of Art, University of Edinburgh. He studied landscape architecture, urban planning, and comparative literature, and has taught at Cornell University, the University of Oregon, and the Amsterdam Academy of Architecture. He is the author of *Go With Me: 50 Steps to Landscape Thinking* (2013) and *Walls: Enclosure and Ethics in the Modern Landscape* (2014).

✚ EDUCATION

Open any recent copy of *Landscape Architecture Magazine* and you come face to face with a world going to hell. Tales of crisis and calamity abound. The September 2014 issue, for example, confronts the reader with the "agony"[1] of drought in California, the "trauma"[2] of Mexico's drug war, and the "fear"[3] of rails-to-trails projects in the United States. Even the public park (Chicago's Lurie Garden is nice but "does have its flaws"[4]) offers little respite from the general gloom. It would seem that there is a great deal to worry about. But it is not the individual chords of the lament that strike one—we have heard those many times before—it is the backbeat of moral injunction that runs beneath them. Don't just sit there, landscape architect! Rise up and seize the challenge! There is no time to waste in the "quest to save"[5] endangered species, eroding coastlines! Our efforts may pale beside the problem, but professional deontology demands that we make them nonetheless. Like a doctor giving a risky drug to a dying man, we are bound by oath to *do something* for patient Earth. After all, we just might find "salvation in a grain of sand."[6]

This oath to save has produced its own distinct form of psychic discomfort in the contemporary practice of landscape architecture. It is different from the pain endured by creative artists, which derives from the terror of making something—*anything at all*—out of nothing. It is also different from the torment of architectural education, which prepares students for the ignominy of a working life marked by long hours and low pay. No, the pain of the landscape architect is something else entirely. Ours is the pain of moral ardency, the anguish that derives from our fervent desire to redeem a fallen world. Like medieval flagellants, we do penance for the original sins of our species (agriculture, money, technology), shoulder guilt for the misdeeds of our predecessors. We groan under the burden to repair, reconnect, reclaim, restore, regenerate, and revitalize, adopting places lost, poisoned, abused, discarded, or forgotten. Visions of apocalypse bring us a strange and often poorly concealed *Schadenfreude,* confirming our sense of doom but promising growth in demand for our services. More than any other design professionals we fancy ourselves

lone visionaries, speakers of truth in a world of lies, guides on the path toward deliverance. We matter (the incantation would go, were it ever sung aloud) not merely because we see and solve 'problems,' but because we are *right.* More even than specialized knowledge or technical skill, this rightness is the good we hawk in the global marketplace, where the sign on our tent reads: VIRTUE FOR SALE.

This is serious business, to be sure. But are we not allowed some *fun*, too? Does our pain for the world, our knowledge of apocalypses to come require us to forego *pleasure* altogether? If the things that we design are to delight as well as redeem, surely we ourselves should be able to delight in the process of making them, and to infect others with this same delight? But we *are* fun! comes the objection. It is just that pleasure must be *useful*, the means toward the morally legitimate end of persuading the (well-meaning but benighted) public to attend to those things that *really* matter: sea-level rise, species extinction, drought and desertification, peak oil, the obesity epidemic, the anomie and isolation of smartphones, and celebrity pornography. There is far too much to be done amid this catalogue of ills for *mere pleasure*, especially when such pleasure might implicate us in the very pathologies we purport to cure. We are prone to lament the disappearance of landscapes of play (yet another modern ill), but only for children. For the rest of us, banished as we are from that garden forever, landscapes must educate, enlighten, edify, redeem. So there we landscape architects stand, perched on a wobbly crate in the town square, delivering our lugubrious sermon to an indifferent world as it rushes past to the Apple Store.

But if we think disavowal of pleasure will raise our prestige and expand our influence, we would do well to think again. As any principled but failed politician will confirm, pained sanctimony risks undermining the very ideals in whose name it is adopted. For one thing, it raises suspicion among a citizenry grown weary, and wary, of moral crusaders – whatever their professed aims. For another, it undermines creativity. Romantic myths of the artist aside, pain generally *depletes* rather than enhances the capacity to wonder and delight at the world. It saps our confidence, silences our intuition, and reduces our willingness to risk and innovate. All this makes it *harder*, not easier, to give the mind that license, that *play* necessary for creative practice. Worst of all, though, is what pain does for our relationships with other people. The body in pain, Elaine Scarry famously noted, is a shrunken body, loosed from the social world, a dweller in a distant land with which lines of communication are damaged or broken. It is a body unable to *connect*, to engage in that imaginative exercise, essential for all social life, called empathy.[7]

All this might be fine for a large and prestigious profession, secure in its domain and immune to the vagaries of public opinion. But it is thin ice indeed for a discipline with a relatively small number of members whose utility remains a complete mystery to most people.[8] Do we really not see the danger at our feet? We are on our way to becoming a buzz-kill profession, the reticent but secretly envious wannabe at the party who looks down on the frippery and is left off the list for next time.

What is to be done? There is no single answer, of course, but we might begin by stopping our present headlong march toward positivist shores we will never reach. Let us instead turn around while there is still time and aim for the rock right behind our backs: the *passion to dream and make environments of sensory bliss* that drew many of us to landscape architecture in the first place. However we may bristle at the thought, it is *this*–not 'evidence-based design,' not 'landscape performance,' and certainly not moral uplift–that society continues to expect of us. Our value does not lie in our capacity to create landscapes that forestall or avert global catastrophe, or to restore what has been lost. It is hard, even heartbreaking to bear, but what is lost is almost surely lost forever, and far more is poised to follow soon. Our value lies instead in our capacity to imagine and create places that elicit joy, pleasure, passion, and wonder *despite this*. For it is the small, ultimately aimless pleasures these places offer–a child's laugh, the splash of water, the scent of dry grass at dusk–that make life still worth living. If this discipline has any moral core, if we stand for anything at all, surely it is this.

Landscape architecture is about well-lived lives, lives that unfold in the company of others, human and nonhuman, amid air and light and warmth, free from sickness and ugliness and alienation and want. Whatever pain we may feel apprehending a world where the rights to these basic things are denied to so many, we must continue to take joy and pleasure in them – not because we must forget, but simply because others take this joy in conditions far less propitious than our own. And part of this joy, this *pleasure despite it all*, is the joy of being silly, unseemly, obsessive, excessive, illogical, gauche, wasteful, and childish.

It is being able to embrace with equal abandon the amusement park and the park, the boardwalk at Coney Island and the boardwalk through the wetland, all the while insisting on the legitimacy of both. If this discipline is ever to amount to anything more than a footnote to apocalypse, we must start to wear our pleasure–in materials, shapes, colors, sounds, smells, memories, the fellowship of friends, and the voices of strangers–on our sleeves. We must start to shout, and show by our own example, how pleasure is the most serious, the most *radical* thing in this broken but still miraculous world. Before we do any of this, though, we must cast off the yoke of moral rectitude once and for all. We must descend from our decorous heights back whence we came. Down there, in the marvelous realm of the senses, in the mire and muck of life–improbable, pointless, glorious, irreplaceable *life*–we will rediscover not only ourselves but our profession.

1 Bill Marken, "Run Dry," *Landscape Architecture Magazine* 104, no. 9 (2014): front cover.

2 Jimena Martignoni, "The Middle of Trauma," ibid., 87.

3 Silas Chamberlin, "The Other End of the Tracks," ibid., 124.

4 Thaïsa Way, "Chicago Fell in Love," ibid., 116.

5 Kevan Williams, "Have Tree, Will Travel," ibid., front cover.

6 Mac K. Griswold, "Salvation in a Grain of Sand," ibid., 96.

7 Elaine Scarry, *The Body in Pain: The Making and Unmaking of the World* (New York: Oxford University Press, 1985).

8 As of May 2013, there were only an estimated 16,330 practicing landscape architects in the United States: US Bureau of Labor Statistics, "Occupational Employment and Wages, 17-1012 Landscape Architects," http://www.bls.gov/oes/current/oes171012.htm (accessed October 26, 2014).

C. MICHAEL HALL, JOERG FINSTERWALDER, YAEL RAM
SHAPING, EXPERIENCING, AND ESCAPING THE TOURIST CITY

C. Michael Hall is a Professor in the Department of Management, Marketing and Entrepreneurship at the University of Canterbury, New Zealand. He also holds positions as Docent at the University of Oulu, Finland, and Visiting Professor at Linneaus University, Sweden. He has published widely on tourism, regional development, and environmental change.

Joerg Finsterwalder is a Senior Lecturer in the Department of Management, Marketing and Entrepreneurship at the University of Canterbury, New Zealand, with special interests in services marketing and temporary urbanism.

Yael Ram is a lecturer in Ashkelon Academic College, Israel, and one of the lead authors of the *Israeli Ecosystems National Assessment*. She works in the fields of psychological aspects of tourism and sustainability.

✚ TOURISM, MARKETING, ECONOMICS, URBANISM

Tourism is one of the most significant factors in cultural, economic, and environmental change. Although popularly understood in the context of vacationing, tourism encompasses all forms of voluntary temporary mobility outside of an individual's home environment.[1] Travel for the purposes of business, visiting friends and relations, health, education, and traditional pilgrimage are as important as leisure and pleasure tourism and usually share the same accommodation and transport infrastructure. The various architectures of tourism, therefore, are not necessarily predicated on designing for pleasure alone: they are designed for consumption.

Globally there are now over one billion international tourist arrivals per year. When domestic travel is also considered, then the number of tourist trips per year will soon exceed the world's population.[2] With tourism growth forecast to continue for the foreseeable future, its significance for place production will continue to expand (see table opposite).

Designing for tourism is primarily concerned with the attraction of the mobile, mainly the tourist, but in the longer term it is also about attracting capital and even migrants (of the right kind) through place promotion.[3] Yet place marketing is not just about the imaging of place, it is grounded in the commoditization of communities and the (re)development of locales for external consumers.[4] In some cases this means designing and constructing new spaces of consumption, especially in non-urban areas where coastal ecosystems or agricultural lands are converted to resort and holiday home destinations.[5] In other locations, existing places (such as former heavy industrial areas that have been made redundant by technological and economic change) are reconfigured or rejuvenated as centers for tourist consumption.[6]

Tourism is therefore embedded in processes of urbanization in at least two fundamental ways.[7] First, as the main driver of urbanization in places that possess very specific urban tourism and leisure production spaces: what is described as 'tourism urbanization.' Second, as an element of consumptive leisure production in commodified urban space in which, although certain parts of urban land use are geared towards satisfying tourism consumers and leisure mobility, the urban economy is not dominated by tourism and leisure production. This could be categorized as 'urbanization tourism' and is further discussed below.

With the exception of resort enclaves, tourism is only one of a number of economic functions in urban centers. However, for many commentators the exemplar tourism-oriented spaces of pleasure are to be found in the form of the 'mass tourism' landscapes of the Mediterranean coast, such as the Algarve, and centers such as Hawaii and Las Vegas, or their replicants in locations like Macau. It is important to emphasize that such tourism urbanization is not new and has its antecedents in the seaside resorts of the 19th century.[8] What is new is their size and market reach. What is now different—and what characterizes the 'new urban tourism' of the 21st century—is the scale, complexity, and diversity of consumption experiences that now exist in urban landscapes built specifically for tourism and leisure as a result of processes of space–time distanciation, via air connectivity and cost reduction, and increased levels of disposable income. Such spaces are generally:

- *Spatially and functionally different* from other urban places. For example, the amenity-driven nature of coastal tourism means that its design is highly linear.

- *Symbolically different*, with various images and symbols as well as a commodified urban environment being used to promote the tourist function. (Although many aspects of the urban environment, including building design, have become shared between tourist destinations as part of the international travel of design ideas together with the consultants that promote them so that an international tourism vernacular can be seen in many resort areas.[9])

- *Characterized by rapid population and labor force growth* in the early stages of urban development. However, the population and labor force tends to have a relatively high degree of transience, underemployment, and unemployment as a function of construction cycles and the highly temporal nature of tourism consumption and production.[10]

- Because of the significant variations in tourist demand over time, they are *characterized by highly flexible forms of production* with respect to space; for example, delineation of day and nightscapes, as well as temporary urbanism in the form of events, festivals, and temporary servicescapes.[11] Spatial flexibility is matched by flexibility in a labor force organized to meet daily, weekly, and seasonal changes in consumption. This is evidenced in high rates of part-time and casual employment, use of migrant labor and minorities, a highly gendered work force, and low rates of unionization.[12]

- *Dominated by state intervention* that has a 'boosterist' tendency, whereby government indirectly and directly invests in infrastructure, such as airports, conference and events centers, stadia, and cultural facilities, with a view to encouraging further inward investment.[13]

- *A foci of transport networks* because of the need to import goods and services, including substantial importation of food, water, and energy from outside the region in order to meet the demands of a highly seasonal population.[14]

GLOBAL INTERNATIONAL + DOMESTIC TOURIST ARRIVALS 2005-2030

	YEAR/BILLIONS				
	2005	2010	2013	2020	2030
ACTUAL ARRIVALS / EST. NUMBER OF INT'L ARRIVALS	0.80	0.94	1.09	1.36	1.81
APPROXIMATE ARRIVALS / EST. NUMBER OF DOMESTIC TOURIST ARRIVALS	4.00	4.70	5.45	6.80	9.05
APPROXIMATE ARRIVALS / EST. NUMBER OF TOTAL TOURIST ARRIVALS	4.80	5.64	6.54	8.16	10.86
APPROXIMATE ARRIVALS / EST. GLOBAL POPULATION	6.48	6.91	7.16	7.67	8.31

NOTE: ACTUAL AND ESTIMATED FORECASTS ARE BASED ON UNITED NATIONS WORLD TOURISM ORGANISATION AND UNITED NATIONS DEPARTMENT OF ECONOMIC AND SOCIAL AFFAIRS POPULATION DIVISION DATA.

LA RIVIERA ITALIENNE
PORTOFINO PRÈS DE S.MARGHERITA ET RAPALLO

YELLOWSTONE
NATIONAL PARK
U.S. DEPARTMENT
OF THE INTERIOR
NATIONAL PARK
SERVICE

GOV. TOURIST DEPT.
MT COOK
NEW ZEALAND

...TRIA
TRAVELING AGENCIES

his hunting ground
of yesterday
NATIONAL PARKS

VENISE ET LE LIDO

SEE AMERICA
WELCOME TO MONTANA
UNITED STATES TRAVEL BUREAU

TASMANIA
The
SWITZERLAND of the SOUTH
Information from
Tasmanian Government Tourist Bureau
Hobart, Tasmania,
or from branch offices in the Capital Cities of the
Australian Commonwealth

Switzerland
ALPINE POSTAL MOTOR COACHES

THE ELECTRIC
ST. GOTTHARD LINE

NEW ZEALAND
THE PLAYGROUND OF THE PACIFIC
GET IN THE QUEUE
FOR
Queenstown

ITALIA TRAFOI PASSO DELLO STELVIO

JUNGFRAU-RAILWAY
11,400 feet a.s.l.
BERNESE OBERLAND
SWITZERLAND

PARIS - LYON - MEDITERRANEE
EN TARENTAISE
PRALOGNAN & LE MASSIF DE LA VANOISE

THEY LIKE WINTER IN NEW YO...
THE STATE THAT HAS EVERY...
BUREAU OF STATE PUBLICITY - CONSERVATION DEPT.

AMERICA
...TES TRAVEL BUREAU

Samoljot bir saat ucqan Jolni karvan
bir kun, hafta va bir ajlab juradi.
ГДЕ САМОЛЁТ
ПРОЛЕТАЕТ ЧАСЫ
КАРАВАНЫ ИДУТ
НЕДЕЛИ

Mitre Peak, Milford Sound
NEW ZEALAND

GILLELEJE
SOL · LUFT · VAND

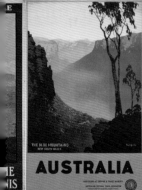
THE BLUE MOUNTAINS
NEW SOUTH WALES
AUSTRALIA
AUSTRALIAN NATIONAL TRAVEL ASSOCIATION

なら
會協光観良奈

SEE AMERICA
UNITED STATES TRAVEL BUREAU

VISIT
PALESTINE

ITALIAN LAKES

FURKA-
OBERA...
BRIG-GLETSCH
ANDERMATT-DISENTIS
SCHWEIZ - SW...

...TURIST SERVICE

INDIAN STATE RAILWAYS

WESTERN AUSTRALIA
TO
Wandering Weir
by
TRANS-
AUSTRALIAN

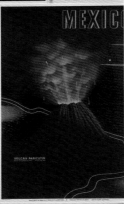

1 C. Michael Hall, *Tourism: Rethinking the Social Science of Mobility* (Harlow: Prentice-Hall, 2005).

2 C. Michael Hall, "On the Mobility of Tourism Mobilities." *Current Issues in Tourism* (2015) doi:10.1080/13683500.2014.971719.

3 Edward J. Malecki, "Jockeying for Position: What it means and why it matters to regional development policy when places compete," *Regional Studies* 38, no. 9 (2004): 1101–20.

4 Johan Hultman & C. Michael Hall, "Tourism Place-Making: Governance of locality in Sweden," *Annals of Tourism Research* 39 (2012): 547–70.

5 C. Michael Hall, "Second Home Tourism: An international review", *Tourism Review International* 18, no. 3 (2014): 115–35.

6 Malecki, "Jockeying for Position."

7 Patrick Mullins, "Tourism Urbanization," *International Journal of Urban and Regional Research* 15 (1991): 591–607; C. Michael Hall, "Tourism Urbanization and Global Environmental Change," in Stefan Gössling and C. Michael Hall (eds), *Tourism and Global Environmental Change: Ecological, Economic, Social and Political Interrelationships* (London: Routledge, 2006), 142–56.

8 C. Michael Hall & Stephen Page, *The Geography of Tourism and Recreation: Environment, Place and Space* (Abingdon: Routledge, 2014).

9 John B. Jackson, *Discovering the Vernacular Landscape* (New Haven: Yale University Press, 1984).

10 Hall & Page, "Geography of Tourism and Recreation."

11 Sarah Bonnemaison & Christine Macy (eds), *Festival Architecture* (London: Routledge, 2007); Peter Bishop & Lesley Williams, *The Temporary City* (London: Routledge, 2012).

12 Hall, *Tourism: Rethinking the Social Science of Mobility.*

13 Doris Schmallegger & Dean Carson, "Whose Tourism City Is It? The role of government in tourism in Darwin, Northern Territory," *Tourism and Hospitality Planning & Development* 7 (2010): 111–29; Michael Woods, "The Local Politics of the Global Countryside: Boosterism, aspirational ruralism and the contested reconstitution of Queenstown, New Zealand," *GeoJournal* 76 (2011): 365–81.

14 Miku Dixit, "Departure Gate Urbanism," *Log* (2010): 29–36.

15 Hall, "Tourism Urbanization and Global Environmental Change."

16 Stefan Gössling, et al., "Tourism and Water Use: Supply, demand, and security. An international review," *Tourism Management* 33 (2012): 1–15.

17 Stefan Gössling, C. Michael Hall & Daniel Scott, *Tourism and Water* (Bristol: Channel View, 2015).

18 C. Michael Hall, "Global Change, Islands and Sustainable Development: Islands of sustainability or analogues of the challenge of sustainable development?" in Michael Redclift & Delyse Springett (eds), *Handbook of Sustainable Development* (Abingdon: Routledge, 2015).

Tourism urbanization tends to be focused in high-value-amenity environments and is closely associated with other forms of amenity-related urbanization such as retirement migration. The impacts of such developments are particularly pronounced in coastal areas where tourism has, in effect, received a substantial environmental subsidy. The Mediterranean coastline is one obvious example of a landscape transformed by population and tourism development pressures. At the turn of the 21st century over 43% of the Italian coastline was completely urbanized, 28% partly urbanized, and less than 29% free of construction. Similar rates of coastal urbanization are also to be found elsewhere in the region. For example, in Cyprus 95% of the tourism industry is located within two kilometers of the coast.[15]

The loss of dune systems and wetlands together with seasonal pressures on water and sewage place coastal ecosystems and biodiversity under severe stress. The direct and indirect water demands of tourism can be substantial, leading to increased competition with other sectors such as farming, and often requiring the importation of water or the development of desalination plants.[16] This seasonal demand also leads to significant seasonal outflows of waste, often overwhelming local infrastructure. In the Mediterranean, only 80% of all wastewater from both residents and tourists is collected in sewage networks, only half of which are connected to wastewater treatment facilities. Untreated sewage continues to be discharged into the sea. Inappropriate siting of tourism facilities and infrastructure on foreshores, dune systems, and wetlands can also exacerbate the impact of wastewater.[17]

Although the infrastructure of tourism urbanization in the form of airports and roads tends to be undertaken through central and local state initiatives, the less spectacular (but no less important) aspects of water and sewage services provision are often left behind. In great part this is because of the issue of who should pay. In many countries the permanent population of a destination has to bear the costs of developing services for the tourist high season, at which point the effective population of a resort area may be three or four times higher than the permanent population. Yet, if destinations are primarily competing to attract visitors on the basis of cost, then government and industry may be loath to pass on the expense of services provision to the tourist. Many specialized tourist destinations may similarly be limited in public transport provision or designed to make them more walkable and instead focus on car mobility in linear urban zones.

The above description of tourism urbanization may seem bleak. Yet destinations do undergo transformation and can potentially diversify over time. If they don't, then given the changing fashions of tourist taste, as well as the even more important changing dimensions of accessibility and cost, they then fade as resort destinations, and plant and infrastructure age. In such cases the availability of relatively affordable (former tourist) accommodation may attract other mobile populations, including retirees. Former resorts close to major metropolitan areas may also become commuter centers or even become part of larger conurbations.

In less developed countries, and especially small island states, the growth of resort centers is problematic in the longer term because of the limited range of redevelopment opportunities and reliance on tourism as a means of employment generation and foreign exchange earnings. The issue for such countries is how to develop tourism without simply competing on the basis of price, especially given the extent to which characteristics of sun, sand, and sea are readily substitutable. In such cases, low-cost tourism products may become the leisure economy equivalent of clothing sweatshops. One possible direction is to focus on biodiversity and cultural heritage as distinguishing product features. However, such measures require careful husbandry of resources at a time of population growth and rising expectations, while concerns over climate change and sea-level rise make the long-term prospects for some coastal and island resorts highly problematic.[18]

In urban centers that predate the modern leisure economy, tourism and the creation of spaces of pleasure consumption have become integral to the shaping of cities, whether as part of the quartering or rejuvenation of older districts as part of regeneration strategies or in the development of 'new' precincts, often as part of the replacement of derelict brownfield sites.[19] The combination of conference center, retail, hotels, restaurants, apartments, and cultural space has become ubiquitous to urban waterfront redevelopment strategies that seek to attract local and foreign middle-class leisure consumption. The construction of such serial space is deliberately focused on the creation of temporary and 'permanent' spaces and structures in which the visitor can experience consumptive pleasure. In such settings, local people become integral to the authenticity and attractiveness of the place because of their contribution to the atmospherics of the tourist experiencescape.[20]

In the contemporary neoliberal economy, in which emphasis is placed on market values, tourism may serve to assist in the conservation of heritage and the built environment. Place identities that have developed over time may prove valuable to the tourism industry as urban regimes seek to differentiate themselves. Heritage architecture and streetscapes can prove more authentic and attractive than yet another conference center. In some cases, tourist interest in the local may even encourage residents to rediscover and value elements of their own city. In a wider context, tourism and hospitality is critical to urban development, innovation, and well-being because of its vital support role for business, connectivity, and quality of life. So long as they are not just perceived as tourist space, cultural quarters and cultural and entertainment districts are just as important for residents as they are for visitors.[21]

Successful urban development that is responsive to community and industry needs therefore must be able to integrate tourism within sustainable urban planning rather than treat it in isolation. Although tourism is a global phenomenon, it is experienced locally and, in the contemporary mobile economy, we are arguably all tourists now. Embracing the local and minimizing the serial monotony of design globalization may therefore increase the likelihood of win-win scenarios in which tourist and local satisfaction with the urban environment is increased. Therefore, sustainable urban design practices that put a value on the legibility of place, the capacity to move around a city by public transport and on foot and bicycle, and which enliven and value public space can create a positive consumer habitat valued by local and tourist alike.[22] In the long run, the most sustainable tourist destinations are not ones that rely on tourism alone, but are living, working, and diverse communities that allow their distinctive identities to evolve over time and, though welcoming of visitors, focus primarily on meeting their own needs.

19 C. Michael Hall, "Servicescapes, Designscapes, Branding and the Creation of Place-Identity: South of Litchfield, Christchurch," *Journal of Travel and Tourism Marketing* 25, no. 3 (2008): 233–50; Marichela Sepe, "Urban History and Cultural Resources in Urban Regeneration: A case of creative waterfront renewal," *Planning Perspectives* 28 (2013): 595–613.

20 Tom O'Dell & Peter Billing (eds), *Experiencescapes: Tourism, culture and economy* (Copenhagen: Copenhagen Business School Press, 2005).

21 Hall, "Servicescapes, Designscapes, Branding."

22 Anna Strandell & C. Michael Hall, "Impact of the Residential Environment on Second Home Use in Finland – Testing the Compensation Hypothesis," *Landscape and Urban Planning* 133 (2015): 12–33.

EUROPE

Spain

France

Italy

Venice

Greece

Ireland

Great Britain

Oslo

Norway

Finland

Switzerland

Sweden

Europe Main Island

St. Petersburg

Monaco

Germany

GREENLAND

Nuuk

Kapisillit

Tasilaq

Arsuk

Narsarsuoq

Cape Farewell

Kap Bridgman-
Cape Morris

Siorapaluk

Nord

Independence

Pituffik-York

King Wilhelm

Peary Land-
Danmark Havn

Ilulissat

Upernavik

Godhavn

Attu

King Christian IX

Davis

Daneborg-
Mont Forel

Frederick -
Jensun Nunatakker

RUSSIA

Moscow

Rostov

Georgia

Archangel

Novaya Zemlya

Perm

Murmansk-Vaigach

Orenburg

Azerbaijan

Kazkhstan

Nyda-
Yamal-Surgut

Kemerovo-
Barnqui-Darham

Omsk

Semey

Dikson

Khatanga

Norilsk-Yessey-
Novoryhbnoye-Tura

Ust Port

Yukta

Kezhima

Strelka

Bratsk

Bulun-
Yakutsk-Olenek

Faina

Zeya

New Siberia

Tiksi-Vladivostok

EAST ASIA

Mongolia

Hotan

Lhasa

Mt. Everest Island

Katmandu

Belogorsk-Nanjing

Sapporo

Tokyo

Korea

Japan

Shanghai

Beijing

Singapore

Hainan

Hong Kong

Burma

Thailand

Malaysia

Sumatra

Java

MID EAST / INDIA

Yemen

Iraq

Kuwait

Lebanon

Turkey-Syria

Bahraln

Jordan-
Saudi Arabia-Sinai

Pakistan

Iran

Qatar-UAE-Oman

South India

North India

Sri Lanka

Bangladesh

AFRICA

Egypt

Libya

Eritrea

Sudan-Chad

Ethiopia

Somalia

Moroccao-
Mali-Mauritania

Tunisia-
Algeria-Niger

Liberia

Nigeria

Cameroon

South Sudan-Kenya

CAR-Congo

Tanzania

Mozambique

Zambia

Angola-
Zaire-Namibia

Botswana-South Africa

Zimbabwe

Madagascar

Berkner

Dumont D'Urville

N. AMERICA

Prince Edward

Coats

Newfoundland

Labrador

Quebec

Ontario

Manitoba

Saskatchewan

Alberta

Minnesota

Montana

Iowa

Wyoming

Utah

California

Nevada

Colorado

Illinois

Indiana

Michigan

Ohio

Virginia

Carolina-Georgia

Missouri

Texas

Florida

New York

Baja California

S. AMERICA

Brasilia

Peru

Paraguay

Sao Paulo

Rio de Janeiro

Isla Antilles Mayores

Lesser Antilles

Colombia

Isla Venezuela

Ecuador

Amazonas Island

Guyanas Island

Bolivia

Buenos Aires

Chile-Santiago

Patagonia

Uruguay

Argentina

Tierra del Fuego

Falklands

Coronation

Clarence

AUSTRALIA

Adelaide-
New South Wales

Northern Territory-
Western Australia-Queensland

Victoria-Tasmania

New Zealand

Vanuatu-Tonga-
Tahiti-Bora Bora

Development Status

Unknown ●

Developed

Cancelled

STATE OF THE WORLD

- 3 meters **above sea level**
- 9 km **long x** 7 km **wide**
- 300 islands, **70% purchased**
- 320,000,000 m³ **dredge**
- 34,000,000 tons **of rip-rap**
- 27 km **long breakwater**
- $3,000,000,000 **construction**
- $30,000,000 **avg. per island**

The World Dubai has been quiet since the recession of 2008. Only two islands have been built on since dredging was completed. Lebanon hosts a private beach club that will soon become a larger night club under a new owner. Dubai's Crown Prince, Sheikh Mohammed bin Rashid al Maktoum, built a spec house on Upernavik in Greenland. The island was given to F1 driver Michael Schumacher as a retirement gift and has since been renamed Michael Schumacher Island. Despite the lack of infrastructure for water and electricity, the Austria-based Kleideinst Group is pushing forward with the Heart of Europe.

Consisting of six islands, the development will feature imported European street artists, thousand-year-old olive trees, and snow-lined streets, made possible through German engineering. Sweden will be the first island to open with restaurants and a hotel. This development is encouraging for the rest of The World but how long will the deserted islands last? The ferry company contracted to shuttle visitors to The World has sued the developer, claiming that the channels have begun to silt in and some islands have begun to sink. The impacts of climate change on The World have only just begun to show themselves.

LOOKOUT MOUNTAIN DRIVE
DENVER

ONE DAY IN DENVER'S
NEW
MOUNTAIN
PARKS

PUBLISHED BY
The CITY & COUNTY of DENVER
DISTRIBUTED BY
The TOURIST BUREAU
· 715 SEVENTEENTH ST ·

THE PLEASURE DRIVE

Paul Daniel Marriott is a landscape architect and preservation planner. He is the author of *Saving Historic Roads* (1998) and *Milestones to Mile-Markers* (2004), and is considered a leading expert in the field of historic roads. He is currently completing his PhD in landscape architecture at the University of Edinburgh, where he is researching the origins of pleasure driving.

✛ LANDSCAPE HISTORY, TRANSPORTATION

"Every American who is in the habit of traveling, which is almost equivalent to saying every American..."[1] So begins the first book by English architect Calvert Vaux. His astute observation not only captured the wanderlust of the typical American, but also the popularity of a distinctly new form of travel – driving for pleasure. Vaux, together with Frederick Law Olmsted, designed and planned the first significant pleasure road system in the United States, for Central Park in New York. The well-constructed drives, revealing picturesque scenes and prospects, established both the advanced engineering practices and landscape theories to create pleasure roads in America. Within 60 years, motorcars would be gliding along newly developed automobile parkways modeled on the carriage drives of this great public park.

The automobile parkway has long been considered one of the great contributions of American landscape architecture. Its serpentine alignment, leafy canopy, and elegant bridges were viewed as a civilizing influence on the motorcar in the early decades of the 20th century. Beginning with the Bronx River Parkway in Westchester County, New York, American cities viewed the development of attractive, spacious, and green parkway corridors as a way to connect dense urban populations to the arcadia of mountain parks and recreational areas just beyond the reach of metropolitan regions.

The antecedents of the American parkway may be traced to the development of British pleasure roads at the end of the 18th century. Designed and constructed to engage the user with the landscape, this new road type sought alignments presenting the finest scenery and selected destinations offering the finest views. The pleasure road was a radical departure from the utilitarian approach that guided road development for millennia and its introduction may be traced to a convergence of British landscape theories and engineering advances occurring at the time. By 1800, four factors had emerged and coalesced to make pleasure driving a reality: modern road engineering, advances in carriage design, kinesthetic landscape theory, and the Picturesque Movement.

The Picturesque Movement in Britain established the philosophical (and aesthetic) foundation for pleasure roads in the United States. One of its earliest and most articulate advocates, William Gilpin, encouraged the chattering classes of the late 18th century to abandon the comforts of the Grand Tour for the wild landscapes of Wales, the Lake District in England, and the Highlands of Scotland. In an era when the first modern carriages were manufactured and advances in civil engineering made highways comfortable and reliable, he articulated a novel concept: viewing scenery from a moving vehicle.

Humphry Repton was the first landscape architect to apply Gilpin's concept to the design of new pleasure roads.[2] Establishing his practice in 1788, Repton's design philosophy was influenced by the unprecedented innovations in mobility and communication that were altering the course of travel in Britain.[3] Repton identified a greater application arising from the advances in road-making and the national obsession with picturesque scenery. "It is remarkable," he wrote, "that no attempt should have been made to render objects of so much beauty and variety accessible... from the windows of a carriage."[4] By applying the technological advances in motion to his innate understanding of kinesthesia–"I delight in movement"[5]–he designed pleasure roads as primary features of his landscapes. His oeuvre of executed works and writings established the fundamental design principles for pleasure drives and informed their development in the United States.

Opposite: Denver Mountain Parks Brochure

The rise of the American Picturesque established an appreciation for the American landscape, and celebrated domestic scenery as an embodiment of the democratic values of the new republic. However, due to the lamentable quality of the young nation's roads, accessing early picturesque destinations was an arduous undertaking. In his widely read and influential book, *A Treatise on the Theory and Practice of Landscape Gardening Adapted to North America*, Andrew Jackson Downing introduced Americans to the possibilities of pleasure roads designed in the "modern style" by Repton, a man he called "one of the most celebrated English practical landscape gardeners."[6] Downing, who noted the pleasure drive is "a variety of road rarely seen among us,"[7] envisioned carriage drives as a central feature of the New York public park for which he advocated.

> In such a park, the citizens who would take excursions in carriages, or on horseback, could have the substantial delights of country roads and country scenery, and forget for a time the rattle of the pavements and the glare of brick walls.[8]

Downing never lived to see his vision of Central Park realized. He died tragically in 1852, leaving Calvert Vaux, the architect he had recruited from London, as one of the few architects in America trained in landscape design.[9] Educated in the English Picturesque, Vaux viewed roads as an organizing structure, noting "roads should wind in graceful, easy curves, and be laid out in accordance with the formation of the ground and the natural features of interest."[10] It was Vaux who, in 1857, invited Frederick Law Olmsted to partner with him on a design for "The Central Park" competition.

Pleasure roads were a significant feature of Olmsted and Vaux's winning proposal for Central Park. Their plan continued the tradition of curvilinear alignments and picturesque views advocated by Repton, but also introduced sophisticated vertical alignment that allowed the carriage roads to pass over and under the park's pedestrian paths and bridle trails "by a peculiar system of arched passages."[11] This extraordinary separation of intersections allowed the maximum enjoyment of the park landscape by each user group. Additionally, Olmsted and Vaux depressed the four transverse roads required to carry the city's cross-traffic through the park. The ingenious use of excavated corridors and land-bridges to guide the park's carriage drives over the busy transverse roads established the modern precedent for separating local and through traffic.

The carriage drives of Central Park represented the most highly engineered and sophisticated network of roads in the United States when they opened to the public in 1860. "In fact," effused the *New York Times*, "there is no place in the country, or as far as we have seen in any other, where driving can be so perfectly enjoyed as on the avenues and broad roads of the Central Park."[12]

The romantic drives of Central Park became *de rigueur* for the country parks being developed in America's growing cities. In 1870, recognizing the popularity of pleasure driving, Olmsted and Vaux designed a landscaped corridor and pleasure road as an approach to Prospect Park in Brooklyn – they termed the new road a 'parkway.' It was the first of a new type of pleasure road designed to connect the city's urban parks to one another. The parkway model would be employed to connect Olmsted-designed parks within Buffalo and Boston, and H.W.S. Cleveland-designed parks within Chicago and Minneapolis. In the late 1890s, presaging the auto age, the Metropolitan District Commission in Massachusetts began construction of the nation's first regional parkway system – encompassing both Boston and its growing suburbs.

It can be argued that the exacting standards of landscape architects to accommodate utility and beauty within these highly engineered parkway corridors established a new expectation for public roads in

Above: Henry Hudson Parkway, New York, 1947

America. With the democratization of travel made possible by the mass production of the automobile, landscape architects saw a new opportunity for pleasure roads: connecting the urban working classes to the delights of the countryside. The profession of landscape architecture was poised to lead a new era of highway design.

The first purpose-built roads for automobiles were pleasure roads. Unlike the existing public road right-of-ways quickly macadamized and pressed into service for the motorcar, newly constructed pleasure roads presented unprecedented opportunities for innovation and experimentation. With the speed and scale of the new motorcar, landscape architects reevaluated the kinesthetic relationship between the automobile and the roadside and designed ribbon-like alignments that both ensured safety and engendered admiration.

The Columbia River Highway, completed in 1922, was the first automobile pleasure road constructed within a dramatic landscape setting. Designed by landscape architect Samuel Lancaster, the elegant scenic highway skirted basalt cliffs, leapt deep chasms over razor-thin bridges, and tunneled through rock faces outfitted with viewing windows – all while maintaining an enviable maximum grade of five per cent. The highway proved that modern engineering and modern landscape architecture could take the motoring public to the most sublime of destinations via a beautiful road offering the maximum of safety and leaving the most minimal imprint on the landscape. It would serve as a model for the newly established National Park Service and the first automobile pleasure road constructed in a national park: the Going-to-the-Sun Road at Glacier National Park in Montana, completed in 1932.

In the East, the Bronx River Parkway introduced automobile pleasure driving in a newly reclaimed and restored landscape along the Bronx River. The new parkway dramatically expanded the scale and complexity of its 19th-century urban predecessors. The parkway "was not designed as an important arterial way...Rather, it was planned as a pleasant recreational drive connecting the system of parks in the Borough of the Bronx with the highways surrounding certain reservoirs of the New York City water supply system in Westchester County."[13]

Designed by landscape architect Gilmore Clarke and civil engineer Jay Downer, the Bronx River Parkway established many of the design principles that would come to define the modern highway era. To ensure the primacy of the landscape and maximum pleasure (and safety) for the driver, Clarke limited parkway access to designated entry roads. Many of these roads passed over or under the parkway, separating local traffic from parkway traffic. As with Central Park, Clarke noted, "[w]e found that the engineering part of the work that we undertake is so closely interwoven with landscape and planning...that the two must be developed together."[14] When completed in 1925, the Bronx River Parkway was the most modern highway in the nation.

Landscape architects introduced modern highway engineering into the American landscape through the pleasure road. In the first decades of the 20th century, the parkway was the preferred planning response to the crowded urban arterials and new suburban development rapidly redefining America's cities. Unfortunately, its adaptation to a commuter road gradually diminished the influence of the landscape on its design. As scenic alignments and sublime destinations were no longer essential to its identity, the parkway devolved to the freeway. Nevertheless, the legacy of landscape innovation remains within the separated-grade interchanges and limited-access corridors of our modern highway system – ideas first conceived for the pleasure drive.

1 Calvert Vaux, *Villas and Cottages* (New York: Harper and Brothers, 1864), ix.

2 Repton titled himself a 'landscape gardener,' Calvert Vaux is credited with creating the term 'landscape architect' in 1857.

3 Between 1750 and 1811, journey times between London and major cities were cut by up to two-thirds: Stephen Daniels, *Humphry Repton* (New Haven: Yale University Press, 1999), 27.

4 Humphry Repton, *Blaise Castle, Gloucestershire* (Bristol City Museums: Red Book, 1796), unpaginated.

5 Humphry Repton, *Fragments on the Theory and Practice of Landscape Gardening* (London: T. Bensley and Son, 1816), 235.

6 Andrew Jackson Downing, *A Treatise on the Theory and Practice of Landscape Gardening*, Dumbarton Oaks Trustees for Harvard University, 1991 reprint (New York: Putnam, 1850), 339.

7 Ibid., 341.

8 Andrew Jackson Downing, "The New-York Park," *The Horticulturist* 6 (1851): 347.

9 William Alex, *Calvert Vaux* (New York: Ink, Inc., 1994), 11.

10 Vaux, *Villas and Cottages*, 51–52.

11 Charles Beveridge, *The Papers of Frederick Law Olmsted*, vol. III (Baltimore: Johns Hopkins Press, 1983), 355.

12 "A Day in the Central Park," *New York Times* (April 15, 1860).

13 Gilmore Clarke, "The Parkway Idea," in W. Brewster Snow (ed.), *The Highway and the Landscape* (New Brunswick: Rutgers University Press, 1959), 39.

14 Letter from Gilmore D. Clarke to Philip N. Youtz (November 25, 1925).

SCOTT JENNINGS MELBOURNE
RESORT URBANISM

Scott Jennings Melbourne is an Assistant Professor of Landscape Architecture at the University of Hong Kong. His research advances design implementation methodologies and explores the impact of landscape spaces on urban networks. He holds a BLA from the University of Washington and an MLA with Distinction from Harvard University.

✛ URBAN PLANNING

Hong Kong's Discovery Bay presents an emergent typology for integrating urban growth at significant densities within a rich topographic condition. A mixed-use development primarily devoted to residences, Discovery Bay manifests commercial success even as the collective project highlights risks in combining urban convenience with landscapes of leisure before more comprehensively establishing the social structures of community. Within the context of an increasingly dynamic Southeast Asia, it is critical that successful, if imperfect, developments like Discovery Bay are investigated as living experiments that may inform future growth patterns throughout the region. As a built work with more than three decades of expansion and inhabitation, DB (as Discovery Bay is colloquially known) is also relevant to designers and planners beyond this territory, who may recognize within the development relationships and ideas worthy of adapting to different climatic and economic contexts.

Hong Kong Special Administrative Region is a dense coastal territory with unrealized potential in advancing urban growth that maximizes the opportunities of a richly diverse landscape setting. Constituting a collection of islands paired with an undulating peninsula reaching out toward Southeast Asia, this is a metropolis of coastlines. The city is also a financial center of international stature, offering varying forms of economic opportunity matched with relatively high political stability to historically attract waves of individuals from across the border in the People's Republic of China and beyond. With settlement of these groups constrained by colonial borders, the city today contains some of the highest population densities in the world within a condition aptly described as "a subtropical mountainscape that's equal parts Manhattan and Hawaii."[1] Dramatic topography, where the majority of hillsides are sloped at 20 degrees or higher,[2] places severe limits on buildable areas and gives armature to the city's urban form by guiding the forces of compression and demanding that urban expansion be absorbed within preciously sparse flat collars of shoreline. All the while, building heights have continued to be raised to the point that structures today are commonly built at heights of 40 stories or more. With protected green slopes providing a backdrop, and urban growth abutting waterways with expansive vistas, Hong Kong offers a dramatic example of prospect and refuge[3] at the city scale.

Since the handover of Hong Kong to China in 1997, at which point it gained its Special Administrative Region (SAR)

Discovery Bay is 25 minutes by high-speed ferry from the Central District of Hong Kong.

status, the territory has successfully maintained much of the openness, safety, rule of law, and business-friendly tax conditions that make it a valued center of operations for many foreign organizations and their employees. These foreign professionals, while constituting a relatively minor single-digit percentage of the city's population,[4] maintain higher-than-average salaries and consequently hold an outsized influence on property offerings. Beyond their buying power, these expatriates also carry with them cultural biases and tastes, sometimes differing from what is valued or prioritized in Hong Kong's uniquely hybridized Cantonese culture. While these spatial uses and expectations have traditionally represented a significant example of contrasting values between local and outsider, studies on historic trends in Hong Kong's real estate advertising point to a more recent and pervasive shift in emphasis toward the exterior environments where "[o]pen spaces are mobilized to articulate a prestigious social status."[5]

DB presents the territory's most successful example of a large-scale development that makes use of these pressures and desires, offering what can be described as a secluded kind of "resort urbanism" that is highly prized by its largely expatriate clientele. The community's significant building densities house a population of more than 7,000 residents per square mile,[6] where building blocks are interspersed with a series of open (but, notably, privately managed) spaces taking the form of plazas, pedestrian shopping streets, and even an expansive sandy beach. These more intimate interior environments are complemented by protected upslope greens made accessible by an extensive trail network.

A larger-scale combination of barriers and portals can be used to understand how landscape has been utilized to achieve the resort-like qualities of DB. The development takes advantage of its topographic condition to be situated as an enclave at the eastern edge of Lantau Island, the largest of Hong Kong's islands but one that has traditionally been sparsely populated. For the first two decades of its existence, in fact, there was no vehicular access whatsoever to the DB site, with all construction materials and equipment needing to be transported to the island by ferry. Much as destination resorts make use of choreographed pairings between seen and unseen, served and serving, the resort urbanism of this enclave is supported by calculated juxtapositions of openings and closings, accessible frontages of activity, and rear concealment of supporting infrastructure.

Mass transit plays an essential role, with local bus services augmenting pedestrian connections to help make feasible a ban on private automobile use within the community. This car-free status has a significant impact on the use and character of spaces throughout the development. Meanwhile, regularly scheduled high-speed ferry services play a vital role in facilitating accessibility and making the intensity of Hong Kong's Central District a mere 25-minute boat ride away.

The allure of DB can be understood through an in-person experience of its landscape conditions. An afternoon spent walking the extensive plazas and esplanades of DB makes vividly clear why it has been so financially successful and attractive to its occupants, teeming with families as construction on yet even more housing towers continues apace. There is much on offer for these residents, living in an environment of urban convenience that also takes full advantage of Hong Kong's waterfront orientation and protected green spaces. For a city with already high levels of personal safety (and some of the highest life expectancy levels in the world[7]), DB offers an almost unheard-of minimization of threats. With an absence of personal automobiles, it can feel as though the entire development functions as a playground for children to explore and occupy. This opportunity is especially notable when experienced in the context of greater Hong Kong, where young children are rarely allowed the freedom of unsupervised play. The parents of DB clearly both value such opportunity for their children, and also see this environment as being sufficiently safe for its pursuit. With a baseline of safety having been established, a critical mass of pedestrian activity self-supports the fully domesticated environment. Importantly, this emphasis on safety is internalized, focused on operation and management rather than the kind of reactionary gated communities found in North America or self-contained expatriate compounds constructed in places like Dubai. The place is also distinct from building models found throughout contemporary China where, in cities from Shenzhen to Beijing, a favored typology operates at the superblock scale, locating towers and building podiums at the gated perimeter while maintaining a relatively small private green space at the core. With DB's porous borders and open access, it is not about keeping the unwanted out, but rather the prescription of activities and establishment of ground rules for what is allowed within.

A focus on frontage can be seen in an early masterplan document dating from 1982, where proposed development is concentrated on the waterfront edge and only secondary uses are distributed amongst relatively flat upland plateaus. Access builds from the centrally located ferry pier, with pedestrian paths linking the waterfront program while service roads are relegated to leeward positions. Tellingly, this early masterplan document only labels the Nim Shue Wan village, adjacent to DB's southern edge, without marking existing structures or showing potential paths for accessing and engaging with this fragment of local community.

At the core of DB's physical development is a residential typology that may be identified, contextualized, and potentially applied to other areas exhibiting similar conditions. Within the development itself is an interplay of building mass and open space that offers urban convenience (i.e., a density of public amenities, shopping, and restaurants all within walking distance) together with a variety of designed landscape spaces and access to more

This early Discovery Bay masterplan document describes the development as a resort despite its emphasis on housing accommodations. Courtesy HKRI Ltd.

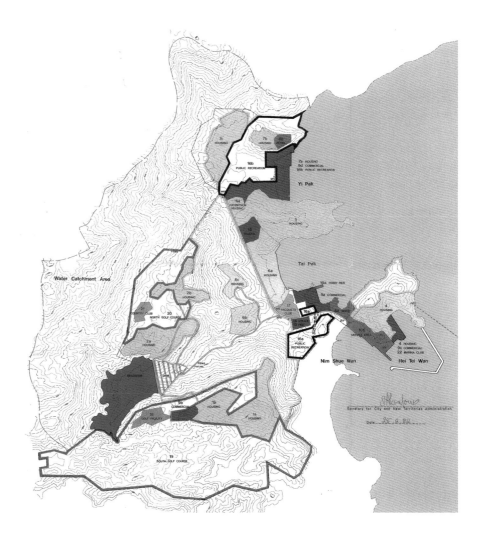

extensive greens that support a spectrum of outdoor activities. This combination of mass and void requires balancing, for with too little development the area will have limited support for domestic activities and lack the gravity to hold users within the village-like destination. Landscape deficiencies will, conversely, make the whole endeavor not worthwhile to those looking for some benefit beyond the city's urban core. Transportation connections are to be convenient and reliable, but focused and not so extensive as to diminish the development's status as destination. Finally, a hospitable climate must be recognized as playing an essential role in supporting such efforts in outdoor living. It is chiefly for this experience of lifestyle that DB's resort urbanism has been pursued: while environmental benefits brought about by heightened housing density and mass transit use are real, these are not differentiating factors within the context of hyper-dense Hong Kong.

Discovery Bay's history sheds light on how this typology emerged as a mix of intentional planning and evolving opportunity. While DB today thrives as a residential outpost, it was not initially intended to function as a bedroom community serving Hong Kong's Central District. The lands were originally zoned for a resort development when long-term lease rights were purchased in the mid-1970s, and have in fact maintained this status until the present day. Shifting from original notions of resort destination to a convenient location for second homes, the development is now firmly established as a desirable residential community. The resulting situation is something of an inverse to what might be found elsewhere: rather than a residential community attempting to take on the air of a resort, Discovery Bay has for some three decades been a resort in designation even though it is home to thousands of residents and had its first hotel open only recently in 2012. The managing corporate owner, Hong Kong Resort Company Limited, embraces this classification in name, and while tax gains generated from the disconnect between zoned and actual usage has in the past been called out as scandalous,[8] the development continues to grow. A variety of mostly local designers have been commissioned to guide DB's development, completing some 14 building phases since the project's inception.

As the development matures, long-term residents have encountered the limits to their influence on decision-making for this corporate-managed community. The lack of representative governance makes the occasional protest or boycott the most visible form of feedback. These activities are sometimes in response to price sensitivity, such as displeasure over fare increases for the high-speed ferry monopolistically controlled by DB's parent company. At other times these modest demonstrations are triggered by operational changes, such as when a popular pub is closed down or a children's facility is, without notice, given over to new management. It is this simmering instability and opaque decision-making that inhibits deep-rooted connections and defines the development's ultimate weakness in functioning as a community. While many occupants of DB will indeed be transitory, others still will raise families and call this place home for many years. During these times of dispute, individuals may be reminded that they are not residents so much as they are customers.

Even as a finely measured mix of isolation and access established the foundation for DB's success, consequential growth is challenging this equilibrium and puncturing DB's sense of isolation. Construction of a new airport, located off the northern edge of Lantau Island and opened in 1998, brought with it increased external infrastructure, including highways and bridges linking Lantau by road and rail to the rest of Hong Kong. The proximity of these developments to DB has demanded that the development's isolation be more self-conscious, increasingly self-imposed, presenting opportunities for ease of access that must intentionally be denied. These connections sometimes prove all too tempting, however, as evidenced by the Discovery Bay Tunnel that opened in 2000, providing direct vehicular links to the nearby North Lantau Highway. This proximity to external threats and opportunities is made all the more clear when comparing the northwestern portions of the early masterplan document with a more current draft version, where not just the North Lantau Highway but also a wastewater treatment plant and the opposing shoreline of Lantau Island itself are shown to be dramatically close to DB. Whereas the void in the earlier masterplan suggested an extreme isolation, the more current document offers a peek around the proscenium at a reality present just offstage.

While the global design community catches its collective breath after China's dramatic rush to development over the past decade and a half, further south the groundwork is being laid for another wave of effort across cities like Hanoi, Jakarta, and even Yangon. In this context, Discovery Bay represents an imperfect exemplar for synthesizing urban form with landscape. As an assemblage it points to possibilities, offering a dramatic example for how landscape at varying scales may be successfully employed in the creation of not only desirable images but also highly livable neighborhoods. And yet, as is the case in all resorts, the messy realities of governance and vital ecologies of life are carefully concealed, here to the point of limiting the place's potential.

1 Evan Osnos, "The Party and the People," *New Yorker* (October 13, 2014).

2 "Natural Terrain in Hong Kong," Hong Kong Geotechnical Engineering Office (accessed 2 October 2014), http://hkss.cedd.gov.hk/hkss/eng/natural_terrain.aspx.

3 Grant Hildebrand, *Origins of Architectural Pleasure* (California: University of California Press, 1999).

4 Hong Kong Census and Statistics Department, "2011 Population Census Thematic Report: Ethnic Minorities," 7.

5 Sidney C.H. Cheung & Eric K.W. Ma, "Advertising Modernity: Home, Space and Privacy 1," *Visual Anthropology* 18, no. 1 (2005): 65–80.

6 As a point of comparison, this density is similar to Brooklyn, New York, albeit with a significantly different massing arrangement.

7 "Hong Kong SAR, China Data," The World Bank (accessed October 11, 2014), http://data.worldbank.org/country/hong-kong-sar-china.

8 Jane Moir, "Discovery Mystery," *South China Morning Post* (January 22, 2005).

ADRIANNE WILSON JOERGENSEN
THE EDGE OF PLEASURE

Adrianne Wilson Joergensen is a designer and researcher at the ETH Zürich Future Cities Laboratory in Singapore. She holds a Master of Architecture from the University of Illinois at Chicago and is currently investigating the spatial and visual products of tourism in the tropics. Joergensen's work has been featured in *SOILED*, *The Economy*, and TheDraftery.com.

+ ARCHITECTURE, URBAN PLANNING

To the tourist, the tropical coastline is the ultimate geography of pleasure. She can easily picture herself relaxing in a lounge chair, watching clear blue waters wash onto white sandy beaches. Her image of the tropics is produced by her vantage point: the seaside resort. Like other contextually oriented architectural typologies, the resort uses siting and window placement to maximize its view. Using *shakkei* methods (Japanese techniques known as 'borrowed landscape'), the self-contained resort "multiplies its landscape dimension" to visually appropriate the surrounding tropical vista.[1] The *shakkei* device most associated with the seaside resort is the infinity pool. Its waterfall edge aligns itself with the coastline, orienting the swimmers' gazes away from each other, towards the horizon and into the sublime.[2]

While the infinity pool's ordering of the natural landscape creates a clear hierarchy between subject and object, its restructuring of an urban setting is more complex. In Singapore, the 495-foot-long rooftop SkyPark infinity pool at Marina Bay Sands (MBS) faces not over the sea, but over the Central Business District (CBD).[3] The experience here is not about a sublime nature; rather, the SkyPark infinity pool directs views back to the city as the pre-eminent object of desire. The singular view from the pool to the CBD is repeated across thousands of tourist photos. An Internet search for 'Marina Bay Sands' yields a remarkably consistent image: pool across the foreground, Singapore skyline in the distance. However, whereas the invisible pool edge at the seaside resort creates an illusory continuity between pool and sea surfaces, the SkyPark pool sharply divides pool surface from vertical skyline.

The difference between the coastal resort and the MBS lies in the agency behind the master-planned vista. Since it has few natural attractions, the Singapore Tourism Board has chosen to emphasize Singapore's appeal as an urban destination.[4] Whereas the seacoast is equated with pleasure in other tropical locales, in Singapore it has been taken over by industry, with only small portions accessible to the public. To make the city appealing as a pleasure destination, the strategy was to create an interior, artificial coastline. Through synthetic urban design, including land reclamation and construction of the freshwater barrage, open sea was transformed into the Marina Bay reservoir.[5]

The Bay is dotted with attractions, including a waterfront park, a floating soccer pitch and stadium seating for national celebrations, a botanic spectacle, art museum, and concert hall. However, the MBS sits on its own peninsula, positioned as a distinct pleasure zone.[6] The MBS houses shopping, eating, and museums in a collection of distinct forms, but the most illicit of its pleasure programs, gambling, is hidden within its expansive base. It is the first such casino-complex to be described as an "integrated resort" – an ambiguous term coined to help smooth its politically charged construction.[7] Its planned segregation from the rest of the CBD may also reflect a Singaporean reluctance, particularly on the part of former Prime Minister Lee Kuan Yew, to allow casinos.[8] The change of heart was driven by a desire to move away from Singapore's "antiseptic" reputation and to remain competitive as a tourist destination.[9]

1   Marina Bay Sands Skypark, with infinity
    pool on western edge
2   Shoppes at Marina Bay
3   ArtScience Museum
4   Marina Bay reservoir
5   Gardens by the Bay
6   Singapore Flyer
7   Helix Bridge
8   Float at Marina Bay
9   Esplanade Theatres
10 Merlion Park
11 The Promontory at Marina Bay
12 Central Business District (CBD)

In its short history, MBS may have become a global icon, but it relies on its urban context as its attraction. This reflexive monumentality implies that there is a dual dependency between the resort and the city. While this connection between icon and cityscape is familiar from more established urban contexts (for example, between Paris and the Eiffel Tower), the intention to redefine the city's image is more explicit here. The effect of showing swimmers at the edge of a rooftop, floating among skyscrapers, is so surreal it becomes its own attractor. Unlike the hidden casino, the ship-like form of the SkyPark, floating atop three towers, 57 stories above the ground, is highly conspicuous. Its edge forms an impressive urban boundary between the working CBD and the peninsula of pleasure.

Both sets of images associate Singapore with pleasure. With its history as a port and British colony, Singapore is and always has been a global city, but with MBS it aspires to attract a global tourist audience. "The motivation for creating a unified 'urban experience' goes beyond aesthetics. The Urban Planning Authority (URA) guidelines described 'an attractive promotional asset that has tangible economic benefits, such as supporting the tourism sector and attracting investment.'"[10] The development of urban spaces is "at once local and global: for any landscape is always

1 Hana Ayala, "Resort Hotel Landscape as an International Megatrend," *Annals of Tourism Research* 18, no. 4 (Beijing: Elsevier, 1991): 576.

2 See description of the tourist gaze, John Urry & Jonas Larsen, "Theories," *The Tourist Gaze* 3.0, Third Edition (Thousand Oaks: SAGE Publications Ltd., 2011): 1–30.

3 "Marina Bay Sands Fun Facts," http://www.marinabaysands.com/assets/Marina%20Bay%20Sands%20Fun%20Facts.pdf (accessed November 28, 2014).

4 T.C. Chang, Shirlena Huang & Victor R. Savage, "On The Waterfront: Globalization and Urbanization in Singapore," *Urban Geography* 25, no. 5 (Singapore: National University of Singapore, August 1, 2004): 212.

5 Lien Sien Chia & L.M. Chou, *Urban Coastal Area Management: The Experience of Singapore: Proceedings of the Singapore National Workshop on Urban Coastal Area Management*, Republic of Singapore, 9-10 November 1989 (Singapore: ICLARM, 1991), 56.

6 This reflects a growing trend among cities worldwide to condense pleasure activities into "consumption compounds," or "large urban precincts built as spectacles." Patrick Mullins, "Tourism Urbanization," *International Journal of Urban and Regional Research* 15, no. 3

both."[11] In light of this agenda, the real monument may be neither the MBS nor the CBD, but the Bay itself. As Singapore's largest freshwater catchment it signifies the country's achievement of first-world status and infrastructural autonomy from Malaysia.

As Kevin Lynch states in *The Image of the City*, looking at the city is a pleasure.[12] However, an urban image is contrary to what tourists expect to see in the tropics, where pleasure is generally associated with images of untouched nature. While the natural coastline of the tropics is extensive, it is a limited resource. As more tourists arrive to experience its exotic natural landscapes, the tropics are increasingly becoming urbanized. The destination's promotional, idealized image of a natural Eden may no longer coincide with its reality. In appropriating *shakkei* methods typically used in natural landscapes, the SkyPark infinity pool represents a new architectural instrumentality for urban tropical destinations. It combines architectural typologies of passive programs–the swimming pool and observation deck–to create new associations between pleasure and urbanity. Its contextual dependency signifies new representational possibilities for urban tropical destinations.

[Surrey: Urban Research Publications Limited, September 1, 1991]: 330.

7 Kah-Wee Lee, "Regulating design in Singapore: a survey of the Government Land Sales programme," *Environment and Planning C: Government and Policy* 28 [London: Pion Ltd, 2010]: 160.

8 Gavin Shatkin, "Reinterpreting the Meaning of the 'Singapore Model': State Capitalism and Urban Planning," *International Journal of Urban and Regional Research* 38, no. 1 [Surrey: Urban Research Publications Limited, January 2014]: 130.

9 Ibid., 128.

10 Kah-Wee Lee, "Feeling like a State: Design Guidelines and the Legibility of 'Urban Experience' in Singapore," *International Journal of Urban and Regional Research* 38, no. 1 [Surrey: Urban Research Publications Limited, January 2014]: 152.

11 D. Mitchell, "The lure of the local: Landscape studies at the end of a troubled century," *Progress in Human Geography*, Vol. 25 [Thousand Oaks: SAGE Publications Ltd., 2001]: cited in Chang, ibid., 416.

12 Kevin Lynch, *The Image of the City* [Cambridge: MIT Press, 1960], 1.

Sources: Shelley Baranowski, *Strength Through Joy: Consumerism and Mass Tourism in the Third Reich* (Cambridge: Cambridge University Press, 2004);
William Cook, "Inside the Holiday Camp Hitler Built," *The Guardian* (August 12, 2001).

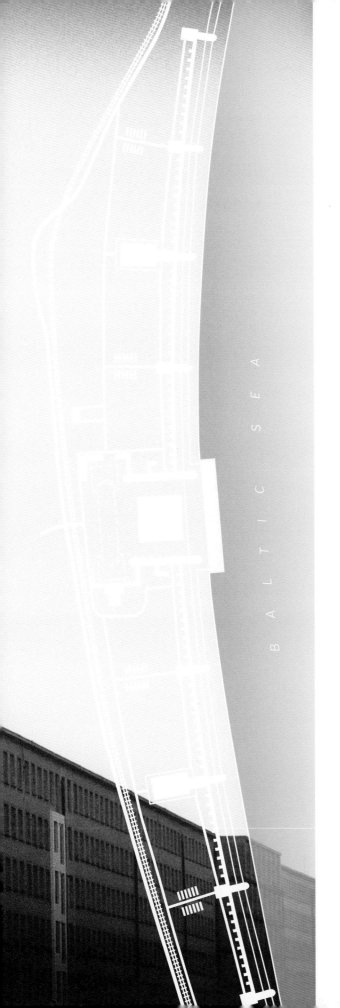

PRORA
KRAFT DURCH FREUDE

Kraft durch Freude (KdF) (meaning "strength through joy") was an organization founded by the German Labor Front of the Third Reich to provide state-sponsored tourism and leisure services to the citizens of Nazi Germany during a time of rebuilding and political instability. By offering tourism packages through a reward-based system, KdF promoted the ideals of self-improvement and edification. These packages were low-cost and highly programmed, thus avoiding conflict with the Third Reich's perception of the hedonism and personal identity associated with market-based consumption.

Prora, located on the island of Rügen, Germany, was the 'poster-child' of the KdF movement. Constructed between 1936 and 1939, it was a testament to the strength of the Third Reich and prototype for five further resorts planned for the Baltic coast. Designed by architect Clemens Kolts, Prora consisted of two complexes, each composed of four utilitarian-style housing blocks, six stories tall, providing accommodation, dining, and recreation facilities for 20,000 German vacationers. Each room, identical in size, overlooked the Baltic Sea to the east. In total, the resort stretched 4.5 km along the northeastern coast of Rügen, making it the largest remaining monument of the Third Reich.

While due to the onset of World War II the resort never saw a single guest, it served as a military barracks, training ground, and hospital for the *Wehrmacht* (Nazi Germany's unified armed forces) and, later, as accommodation for Soviet troops. Currently, Prora houses a youth hostel while another portion is undergoing controversial plans for development as a luxury hotel and condominiums.

Above: A 1939 KdF advertisement for Prora.

MARK RAGGATT

THE AIR WE

BREATHE

MONA, Museum of Old and New Art. Southern facade viewed from Little Frying Pan Island, south of the museum.

Mark Raggatt is an architect with ARM Architecture in Melbourne, Australia.   He is editor of *Mongrel Rapture: The Architecture of ARM* (2014), and curator of *God Knows* at Melbourne University, an exhibit made almost entirely from salvaged Styrofoam.   More recently Raggatt developed a public program and exhibition, *Blue Now: Blue Epoch*, at the National Gallery of Victoria. He teaches design in the Masters of Architecture program at RMIT in Melbourne, where his current series of studios is concerned with impolite dinner conversation, politics, religion, sex, and death, and how architects might respond, if capable.

✚ ART. ARCHITECTURE

Above: The Void and Lift/Stairwell at MONA

Sitting comfortably, I've agreed to proceed; in 15 seconds I will be given a lethal injection. There's a clock counting down in the corner of a dimly glowing screen. In these final moments, not far from me, a man is being sodomized by a blurry but muscular dog. The man's knuckles and knees scrape the floor in awkward subservience. Turning back to the screen I find that I'm dead by my own hand. I don't feel grief or relief, rather something approaching frailty, as if mortality were something small but profound; as if I could hold it in my hand and feel it rustle.

I turn back to the dog and his mate; he is violently and disgustingly beautiful. I'm looking at the *Family of the Future, 9* (1997) by Oleg Kulik. I feel that I'm a creature, not like the dog, but not like the man either. If there is pleasure here, it is extreme pleasure – pleasure at the edge of understanding. The screen glows and others wait their turn. I'm almost slumped in *My Beautiful Chair* (2010), an installation by Greg Taylor and euthanasia activist Dr. Philip Nitschke; besides the armchair, a Persian rug, and a coffee table, there's a Deliverance Machine, designed by Dr. Nitschke to deliver a dignified death to those who want it. I'd been out late in Hobart the night before, drank more than anyone should, and probably said too much. I need some air.

Coming up out of the earth, I feel like Lazarus rising from the tomb, fatigued by death and a little cranky at being woken. Has this been a sacred or profane experience, have I been filled or emptied, am I surfacing satisfied or have I deferred the inevitable? In any case, this deferral allows me to seek out the gift shop. All museums have a gift shop and this one is no different, to get out you have to pass through it, like the gates of hell. This gift shop is in a mid-century modernist house designed by the Australian architect Roy Grounds. The house provides entry to the Museum of Old and New Art (Mona[1]), housed deep underground in Glenorchy, a working-class suburb of Hobart in Tasmania, the poorest state of Australia.

Mona's founder, David Walsh, is a professional gambler, a quixotic, abrupt, torrential, and generous character. Walsh, with best friend Zeljko Ranogajec, leads one of the world's most successful gambling syndicates, the Bank Roll. Mona's collection and the institution itself were built and run with the proceeds of gambling. This is perhaps the least interesting part of Walsh's story. David Walsh is local to Glenorchy, the third child to a marriage turning sour. As Walsh tells it, his parents met in Melbourne, fell in love, divorced their existing partners, married, and moved to Glenorchy. It was there that his mother was reborn in Catholicism via a local priest who told them that God could only recognize their first marriages: they could, however, live as brother and sister. Myra obeyed and Thomas became a violent and violating husband. David was born and the marriage soon failed.[2] Fifty years later, the ashes of David Walsh's violent father rest at the bottom of a museum nearly twice the size of the New York Guggenheim, ostensibly devoted to sex and death. Sex and death are at the extremes of experience, they are Genesis and Apocalypse, but between there is pleasure and pain, and it is this life between that Mona is dedicated to: the extremes of lived experience, the pleasure and pain of being human. I think it was Mark Rothko who said, "If people want sacred experiences, they will find them here. If they want profane experiences, they'll find those too. I take no sides." At least I think it was Rothko, speaking of the *Chapel*, but the sentiment could equally apply to Walsh, and to this strange museum at the edge of the world. The art, the site, the building, and the man who built it all have become a phenomenon.

I need some air.

There are two ways to get to Mona: by road or by river. The MONA ROMA 1, a locally built catamaran, takes visitors up the Derwent River; the city gives way to eucalypts and Triassic sandstone, a hint of the severe yet sublime landscape of Tasmania before a zinc refinery tumbles down to the water; a giant contraption from another time, all steam and pipes, gantries and trusses. Mona can be seen like the refinery's odd twin – it has an ancient bearing, as if exhumed rather than built. In fact, this isn't so far from the truth. The main building that forms Mona–designed by Melbourne architects Fender Katsalidis–has been cut into the peninsula, allowing the building to sit low to the water, an antipodean Petra.

The facade, more like a rampart, is a concrete grid. It recalls road infrastructure, military architecture. The grid is interrupted by rusting Corten steel bastions, there is no suggestion of the interior or clearly defined entry: the façade is not a mask, not intended to conceal, it's just blank, pitiless as if by nature. There is, of course, a fissure through which the visitor must climb between museum and rock. It's possible to run your fingers across stone that has seen mass extinction and the rise of mammals.

The road to Mona takes you through the thinly familiar suburbs of Hobart, spotted with sports fields, a John Deere dealership, road infrastructure, and glimpses of the Derwent River. You arrive, like David Walsh, via Glenorchy. There's a vineyard to the right, part of Walsh's estate, and a sewerage treatment plant to the left, not part of Walsh's estate. There's a large open green which today is ringed in market stalls – a band plays jazz standards, there's a huge barbeque and bean-bags. I grab one and nurse myself with local cider and barbequed pork.

The air smells faintly of shit.

It's time to visit the Cloaca. I head back down to the museum's entrance, crossing an incongruous tennis court–the small orifice formed in the face of Grounds' vivisected house is surrounded by a distorted mirror–the tennis court, the river, and the suburbs are reflected in wobbly concavities. Critics have said that the entry sequence is the most disappointing part of the architectural composition, that the house is cleanly banal compared to the museum below ground. They have missed its necessary banality, it telecasts nothing. But that mirror, like an inverted Claude glass, it focuses the eye and suggests the world below. Concave and indistinct, the mirror reflects the visitor: we are the subject and means of translation. I look at myself – what do I know? The original courtyard of the house has been roofed and a spiral stair takes us down into the rock. Water can be seen seeping through porous stone, running down the walls,

Above: *Snake*, 1970-1972, Sir Sidney Nolan

caught in pebble-filled gutters. Looking up and back as if from the bottom of a well, you can see the belly of the old house, the slab preserved, suspended above, a miraculous excavation.

I still have my 'O' device, a modified iPod touch that acts as Virgil to those touring the depths. The device replaces all those didactic little plaques we all squint at in museums, hoping for a paragraph of revelation. O is not quite like your typical gallery guide, it rarely provides authoritative insight, rather it struggles like us, questioning, proposing, doubting; arguing its way through the world. O knows where you are and where you've been, less like an omnipresent God and more like Hansel and Gretel leaving crumbs along the path, a vain hope for home. If you input your email address, it is possible to retrieve your journey later, to reflect, and to see where you've been. Are we the product of our past?

O represents an attitude that pervades Mona, an attitude that is really at the foundation of the institution. This museum is built on doubt, the kind of doubt that leads to questioning,

subversion, and wonder. Mona, it has been said before, is a modern day *wunderkammer*.[3] It resists the minutiae of classification, reinstating a condition in which categorical boundaries are yet to be defined. The *wunderkammern* were free of the burden to educate, to enlighten, rather the *wunderkammer* was a kind of theater, a machine for association: each exhibit the crystalline beginning of possibilities refracting through adjacency, each a provocation, a dilemma, a doubt. Museums usually take that doubt and replace it with didacticism. Mona relishes in the provocation of doubt.

Joan Littlewood once wrote "19th century society worked on the principle of higher education for a minority and that education was designed merely to perpetuate the status quo; museums and art centres were built 'to form and promote a taste for the beautiful...[and to] humanise, educate and refine a practical and laborious people.'"[4] Mona's zenith is idiosyncrasy rather than universalism. Not educating,

not communicating received truths but manufacturing memory, a kind of prophecy. The *wunderkammer* frees Mona to conflate antiquities and contemporary art, but also to conflate the collection and the building, the site, their marketing, and all of this with the owner. Mona is not just a *wunderkammer*; it is a *gesamtkunstwerk*, a total work of art. Walsh sees a time when the disciplines will highlight the common sources of knowledge; he sees an inverted Tower of Babel in which many things become one.[5]

At the bar, Chinese tourists sit in Victorian furniture drinking wine, teenagers choose lurid macaroons from behind the glass, and I am still heading for the shit machine, the Cloaca. I'm in a ravine between sandstone cliff and blank white wall, a waterfall splashes words drawn from the day's most popular

Google searches. Beyond, people play Ping-Pong on impossibly topographic tables. I pass through gilded galleries, brush red velvet walls, resist the temptation to lick the remains of a suicide bomber cast in chocolate, lose my balance in a labyrinth spelling Gilgamesh, watch the crumbling ashes of a giant Buddha, lust after a paunchy Porsche, and hurry past the casts of many vulvas.

Stopping before 1,620 Sydney Nolan paintings that form *Snake* (1970–1972), a huge rainbow serpent of Aboriginal Dreaming, the awe of creation overwhelms. This is a huge room, in which I and others orbit like wayward moons beneath the constellation of paintings, and above it all I notice that the waffle grid of the concrete ceiling gives way to a skylight; in fact, it doesn't reach the sky but into David Walsh's family home. It is as if he can survey this strange universe and we are given a brief up-skirt glimpse into the heavens above.

It's feeding time' for the Cloaca and I want a good view. Stepping out into the central void of the labyrinth of galleries, a Piranesian stair hangs with perilous dexterity within the concrete grid of column and beam. It sings out a dull clanging note when I step on it, it bounces a little, enough to feel the height should I fall, enough to feel the urge to leap out into the void. The stair reminds me of those diagrams illustrating the tunnels and passages within the pyramids, pointing out to a distant star, burying slaves within. I wonder if this stair points to some greater significance or if it turns back, lacking faith, preferring the travails of the present, the exigencies of circulation. This stair defies the grid, or rather takes advantage of its certainties. The grid is a trope in architecture; it denotes both pragmatism and endless possibility. The grid is democratic, being without hierarchy, the grid is libertarian, being naught but an empty frame. The grid can be pitiless, inexorable, and cruel. The grid, paradoxically, offers liberty and imprisonment. The grid at Mona takes the scale of a giant machine; like Cedric Price's *Fun Palace* [1961], it is an apparatus from which Mona's nightclub-style curation dangles in dark ludic joy, perverse, deathly, funny, democratic, and free. Art and architecture, not as agents of happiness or fulfillment, but of change, of transformation, and therefore of unease.

The Cloaca Professional [2010] by Wim Delvoye is a machine designed to mimic the human digestive system; it hangs suspended, lighting usually reserved for crime drama lends it the air of a reliquary. A gallery attendant appears with a platter and a silver cloche; she has cutlery, and an apron. She moves to a table at one end of the machine, the lifted cloche reveals a meal selected from the museum restaurant. With knife and fork she cuts it into bite-sized portions, feeding the machine. The food is chewed by an InSinkErator,™ and passes down tubes and through elegantly suspended glass vessels. The food is kept at 37.2°C; digested by chemicals, gastric enzymes, and gut bacteria, it is finally excreted, a fetid turd, the sum of great effort.

Great effort, for this Cloaca is one part in a larger *gesamtkunstwerk* that collapses art, branding, gastroenterology, enterprise investment, and plumbing. There is the *Cloaca Turbo*, *Cloaca Quattro*, *Cloaca No. 5*, *Mini Cloaca*, and perhaps it goes without saying, *Cloaca Original.* In 2005, Wim Delvoye issued *Cloaca* bonds at 1.3% interest, apparently guaranteed by the Belgian Banking, Finance and Insurance Commission and

redeemable for cash or feces. Mona, the only museum in the world to own a Cloaca, shares this quality of a total work, a complete enterprise. The Cloaca seems almost a synecdoche for the museum that houses it. It is both a part of the collection and yet represents the whole. Mona is not just the collection, not the building or even David Walsh. Mona is a conglomerate, a singular effort at seeking out human frailty and hubris.

I think of other shit art; Piero Manzoni's little tins, Jacques de Vaucanson's *Digesting Duck*, Pieter Bruegel the Elder's painting with the suspended bum shitting on the globe. But it is the Caganer that seems closest, those little red-capped figures in Catalonian nativity scenes, trousers around their knees, defecating by the babe in a manger. Mona and her Cloaca seem like that, shitting at the edge, a creature of pleasure and pain, silly and serious, blasphemous, subversive, sublime, and profane, pleasure and pain between sex and death.

The air is fine here.

Above: *Cloaca Professional*, 2010, Wim Delvoye

1 David Walsh, *A Bone of Fact* (Sydney: Picador by Pan Macmillan Australia, 2014). While tradition would normally call for the acronym to appear as MONA, David Walsh in his memoir uses Mona, an affectation of the proper noun I have adopted for this essay.

2 Ibid., 16.

3 Peter Timms, "A Post-Google *Wunderkammer*: Hobart's Museum of Old and New Art Redefines the Genre," *Meanjin* 70, no. 2 (2011): 31.

4 Joan Littlewood, "Notes, 1964," in Stanley Matthews, *From Agit-Prop to Free Space: The Architecture of Cedric Price* (London: Black Dog Publishing, 2007). Littlewood does not identify the source of the quotation she references.

5 Walsh, *A Bone of Fact*, 354.

PLAYGROUND FOR A DRUG LORD

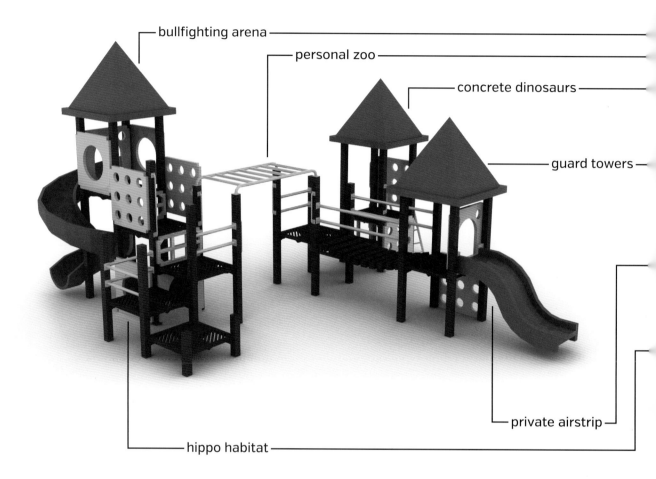

- bullfighting arena
- personal zoo
- concrete dinosaurs
- guard towers
- private airstrip
- hippo habitat

Hacienda Nápoles–the estate of infamous Colombian drug lord Pablo Escobar–was the manifestation of all the pleasures money could buy. Located about 320 km northwest of Bogotá, the 3,700-acre ranch featured a 500-seat bullfighting ring, a children's play park of concrete dinosaurs, and a personal zoo, complete with elephants, giraffes, and hippos smuggled from Africa. The estate also included a private airstrip from which Escobar, at the height of his career, would export some 70 to 80 tons of cocaine each week. The Cessna that carried his very first shipment of cocaine to America is still perched proudly atop the entrance to the property.

For many years following Escobar's death, the estate was left unmanaged and forgotten. The four original hippos in Escobar's zoo multiplied and thrived, resulting in a large herd left to roam unchecked over the estate and neighboring properties. Today, Hacienda Nápoles operates an unusual kind of theme park, combining Jurassic and African themes with a waterpark and a museum housed in the remains of Escobar's former home. Visitors to the park must pass by a maximum-security prison: an irony that one imagines would not be lost on the man who, despite being responsible for the deaths of some 4,000 people, managed to avoid such ignominy during his lifetime.

ABOUT THE DRUG LORD

Known as the 'King of Cocaine,' Pablo Escobar was one of the world's most successful drug traffickers. Reigning over the multi-billion dollar Medellin Cartel for two decades, Escobar allegedly smuggled more than 15 tons of cocaine per day into America and was responsible for ordering thousands of assassinations. Escobar was killed in a gunfight by Colombian National Police in 1993, following a year-long manhunt.

Sources: Mike Ceaser, "At Home on Pablo Escobar's Ranch," BBC News (June 2, 2008); William Kremer, "Pablo Escobar's Hippos: A Growing Problem," BBC News Magazine (June 25, 2014); Kevin Perry, "Drug Traffickers Build the Best Theme Parks," Vice (April 7, 2014).

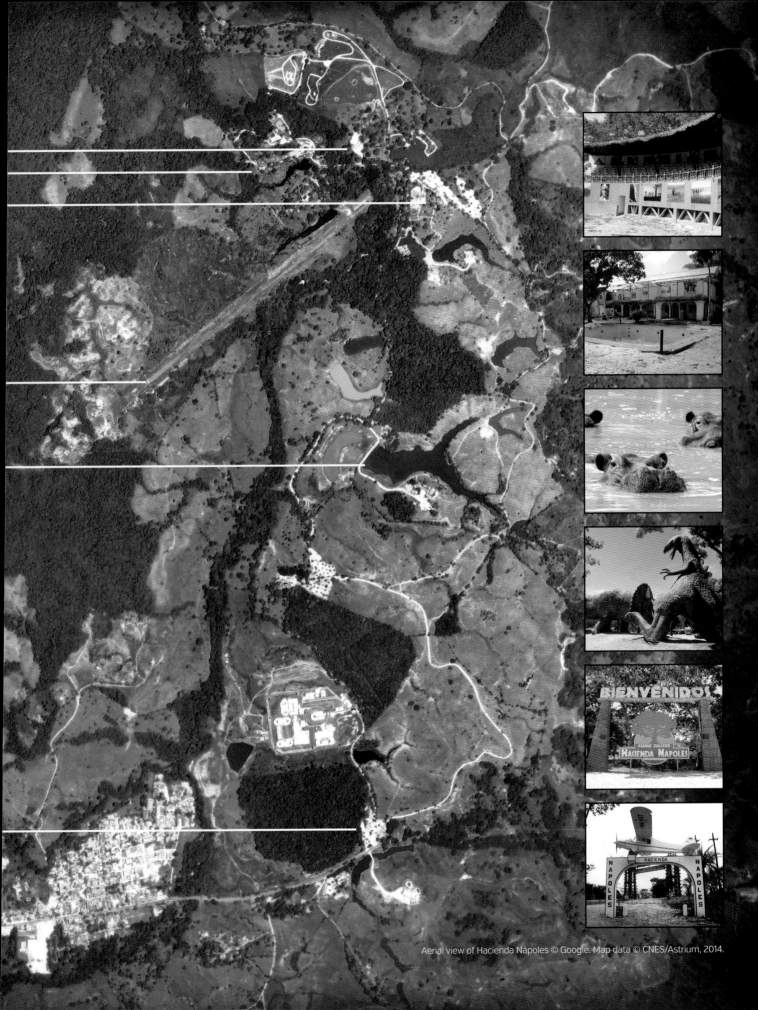

Aerial view of Hacienda Nápoles © Google. Map data © CNES/Astrium, 2014.

PLEASUR

● caviar	● opium poppy
● coca	● sugarcane
● cocoa	● tea
● coffee	● tobacco
● flowers	● wine

This graphic was produced using information compiled from the following sources: Earth Stat; United Nations (UN) Development Programme; Food And Agriculture Organization of the UN; UN Office on Drugs and Crime; International Cocoa Organization; Indonesian Coffee and Cocoa Research Institute; International Coffee Organization; International Flower Bulb Center; the Tobacco Atlas; and the United States Department of Agriculture.

CROPS

IN CONVERSATION WITH VLADIMIR SITTA

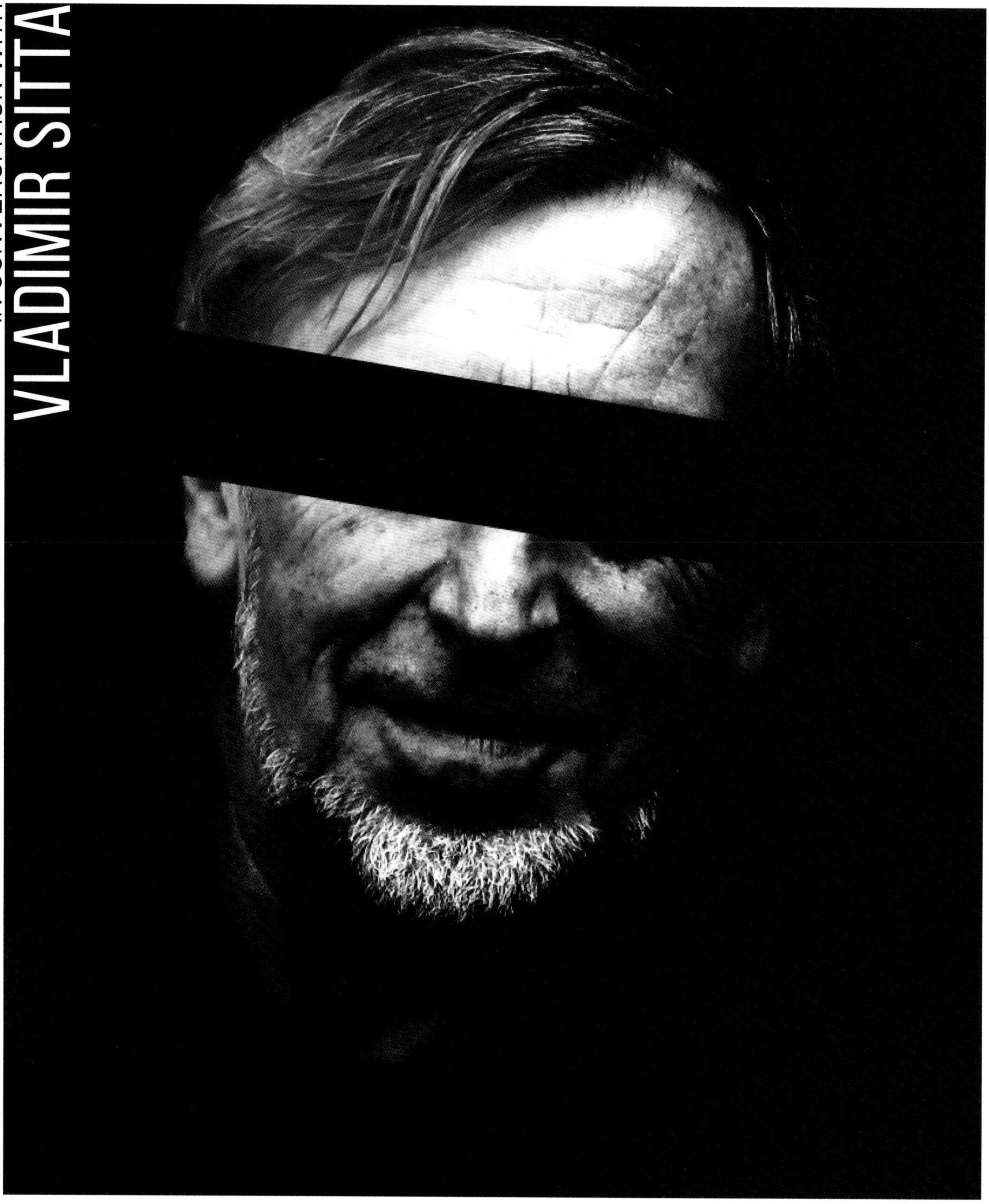

For over 30 years **Vladimir Sitta** has been building small, highly refined gardens for discerning clients. As a rule, in each project he insists on almost complete creative license and pushes materials and construction techniques to their extremes. In seemingly endless combinations derived from his personal sketchbooks, his works typically comprise plants, stone, and water in contorted formations that strike a tension between violent disruption and profound calm. Replete with bones, burnt wood, golden eggs, fire, mist, moss, and other mementoes, his gardens explore a level of sensuality not seen in landscape architecture since the renaissance. LA+ caught up with him in Prague, where he is now leading a new landscape program at Czech Technical University.

+ Do you see your built work as manifestations of your sketches, or are your sketches a separate means of exploring ideas that are unbuildable?

The sketches are a form of forecasting; however, it is not always clear what they are forecasting. Built work, by necessity, censors most of the disturbing aspects that arise in the sketches – not by my intent, but by the controlling power of the client.

They are a form of chaotic diary, occasionally dated but not ordered, unravelling sometimes a tyrannical feeling of repetition. The sketches become more enigmatic as my moods swing, and I may struggle with their meaning at some later time.

+ Is the technical challenge of figuring out how to execute an idea as built form a source of pleasure or frustration?

Pleasure is the condition of endurance. Pleasure and frustration are fused. The frustration is self-imposed; curiosity is real incentive, forcing me to take risks to go to areas unknown to me. The risk is, mind you, usually co-financed by the client, albeit unknowingly.

+ Do you see your gardens as spaces of pleasure for people to enjoy? If so, are they primarily spaces of visual pleasure or are they meant to be experienced in a multi-sensory way?

This is a tricky question. In a way your question has gathered a bit of the dust of time. Our role is changing – from teasing to defending. Ubiquitous surveillance, electronic spying, thermal imaging, drones, and secret installation of monitoring topographies seriously challenge our notion of the pleasure ground. Privacy is becoming a rare commodity that has become difficult to defend, even in the garden. In the future the garden must become a place of the electronic shadow, it must recover the pleasurable dimension that it appears to be losing despite its persisting visual and sensory lure.

+ On the one hand your designs seem to be hyper-controlled and disciplined environments, but there's an undercurrent of disturbance and agitation reverberating throughout these spaces. How does this tension relate to your own personal philosophy on our ability to control nature?

The initial gesture always speaks control, regardless of the form. Design always contains signs of control even if the designer proclaims the opposite. Even if we distribute seeds with the assistance of wind, the controlling hand initiates this process. I don't see my concepts as finite corsets where nature trespasses only by stealth. Ideally an act of undoing would be incorporated into the design. There is, however, the client who is usually interested in the status quo, in freezing a particular moment. On a more personal note, I am a subscriber to enlightened anarchy...but that is another topic.

+ You've referred to your clients as 'victims' and have expected a high degree of latitude in terms of your ability to experiment without interference. Do you generally have autonomy, or are you forced to factor in your client's desires for the project in most cases?

As you know, desire is not a fossilized feeling. It can be influenced and changed. If the client open-mindedly trusts us with the freedom, it forms then an integral part of their desire. I don't particularly like the word forced. It is more my inability to 'white ant' their resolve. I was fortunate to be occasionally engaged by a modern-day Medici. This breed of open-minded people who give you almost absolute freedom is very rare. They should be cloned! I can assure you that it has only a limited relation to money.

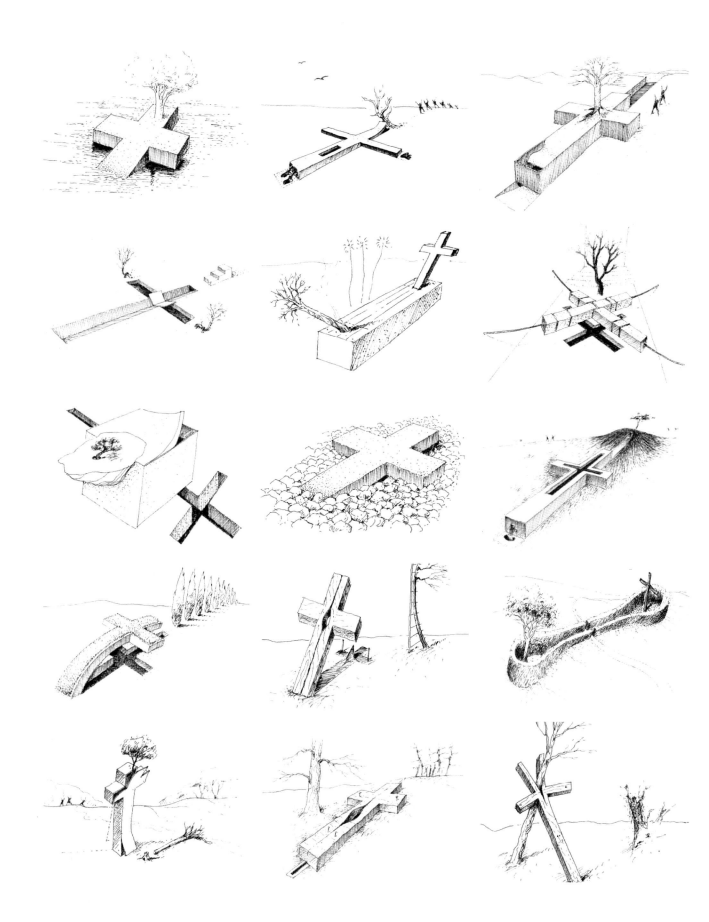

+ Do you tend to see a project as an opportunity to test your ideas and preoccupations at the time, or does the project emerge from a relationship to the particular site and client?

The site is indispensable. Of course there is a whole catalogue of possibilities. We all carry the burden of agendas, collected through our life. To design means to reject most of the collection, to weigh temptation and irresponsibility on one side and cruelty of the time test on the other. The client critiques our work and their acceptance constitutes co-authorship.

+ How has your own background as an immigrant to Australia from the former Czechoslovakia affected your career as a landscape architect?

I don't want to lecture your readers in the political history of Europe; however, in Czechoslovakia we have learnt the art of subtle subversion. Even the landscape could serve then as a medium of dissent. The demise of the Eastern Bloc has dire consequences for democracy. I accept that this statement could appear almost heretical and bizarre to disciples of neoliberalism. I see shocking convergences of past and present political systems that affect even landscape. The landscape had become a vehicle for terror, perpetuated by the state or by individuals. In this context the garden acts almost like an anesthetic. The possibility of paradise seems more remote than ever.

+ Having now returned to Prague, what's the state of landscape architecture in the Czech Republic?

The answer is quite simple: stagnation. This scathing statement needs, however, to be elucidated. I left the country saturated with moral malaise in 1979. There was the ubiquitous secret police and strong state control reaching even into private dwellings. The state was the only client for the tiny profession of landscape architecture. There was only one university teaching landscape architecture in the country of 15 million, admitting only eight to ten students each year. Control of the state, whilst it appeared solid and homogenous, had many cracks hidden from the uninitiated observer. Paradoxically, it was in fact possible to execute some obstreperous designs as acts of defiance.

In the immediate aftermath of the so-called 'Velvet Revolution' in 1989, there appeared to be a lot of optimism and desire to change. A number of neglected public spaces were renovated, but scarcity of good precedents and lack of understanding of how public space is supposed to function often, unfortunately, marred the designs. Sterility enforced by communists has been replaced by sterility by design. Public life does not return to those places simply by changing paving patterns and installing (mostly very uncomfortable) furniture. Freedom to travel and access information led not to an increased awareness of the Czech specificity but to uncritical embracing of global trends of pattern making, fashionable materials, and predictability.

In my opinion, landscape architecture as it is practiced in the Czech Republic now lacks any compelling agenda. Whilst the profession has grown considerably in numbers, it remains intellectually and politically inconsequential. The potential for the profession to be involved in the building and repairing of Czech cities is enormous and is still waiting to be tapped into. Here lies a call to arms for the coming generation of landscape architects. The most important tool they would need is the desire to smash the status quo.

+ And finally, who has influenced you as a designer?

Just a few names: Andrej Tarkovskij, Federico Fellini, Albert Camus, Hannsjörg Voth, Josef Svoboda, and many others make me stand in their shade in the hope of stealing some fragments. Louis XIV and Karl Marx also lurk somewhere.

RICHARD CAMPANELLA
PLEASURE ATLAS

Richard Campanella, a geographer with the Tulane School of Architecture and a Monroe Fellow with the New Orleans Center for the Gulf South, is the author of *Bourbon Street: A History* (2014), *Bienville's Dilemma: A Historical Geography of New Orleans* (2008), *Geographies of New Orleans: Urban Fabrics Before the Storm* (2006), *Lincoln in New Orleans* (2011), and other books. Campanella's work may be perused at www.richcampanella.com.

✚ GEOGRAPHY, HISTORY, PLANNING

As New Orleans' post-Hurricane Katrina recovery of the late 2000s morphed into a rather unexpected economic and cultural renaissance in the 2010s, new faces appeared in new areas, new conversations circulated, and new pleasure spaces began to open. The changes reflect a mounting trend affecting the downtowns of most major American cities, and New Orleans, for all its alleged distinction, is no exception. It is the spatial diffusion of gentrification, and it is drafting the latest cartography in this city's ample atlas of pleasure.

Few American cities make space for pleasure like New Orleans. In some cases the space-making is a byproduct of the architectural past: witness the use of iron-lace balconies, porches, and stoops for relaxing and interacting between private and public space, or the lovely neighborhood squares and neutral grounds (medians) that draw bench-sitters and domino-players. In other cases, spaces are professionally planned for pleasure, as in the case of the Olmsted-designed Audubon Park, the recently beautified City Park, and in the facilities of the New Orleans Recreational Department, which once ranked top in the nation.

More famously, New Orleans' pleasure spaces are products of an ongoing negotiation between an ordinance-wielding municipality acting on behalf of civic order and a particularly revelrous citizenry with a penchant for public festivity. Any given Mardi Gras parade during 'Carnival season,' or festival during 'festival season,' or second line during 'second-lining season' (New Orleans has a distinct sense of time as well as place) abounds with examples of these sorts of spatial pleasures and tensions. The pleasure map–and the calendar–seem to get more and more crowded with each passing year; nowadays, few are the weekends without special events, and many are the weekends

with more than one. But the underlying phenomenon is as old as the city.

New Orleans did not originally find space for pleasure; rather, pleasure found New Orleans. Port cities historically drew a steady stream of transients who, liberated by their anonymity and removed from the responsibilities of home, craved opportunities for gratification in distant entrepôts, to which local entrepreneurs eagerly responded with everything from bars to ballrooms to brothels. Add to this the cultural influences of the so-called Global South, the theory goes, and what resulted in lower Louisiana was a society more inclined to tolerate, and often incorporate, behavior condemned elsewhere. New Orleans' indulgences–'continental Sabbaths,' inebriety, gastronomy, sexuality, miscegeny, musicality–did not form independently or internally, but rather orbited as a social characteristic throughout the global littoral of the 18th and 19th centuries. What distinguished it was its geographical positioning at the northernmost apogee of the South Atlantic–Caribbean subsystem and, after the Louisiana Purchase in 1803, within the expanding borders of the United States – the *southern* United States, a region of traditionalism against which New Orleans' culture of tolerance stood out in stark contrast and set it up for hyperbole and stigma.

New Orleans thus earned an unenviable reputation for debauchery in the minds of other Americans, and written evidence of it can be found ad nauseam in any number of flowery, judgmental 19th-century travelogues and editorials. Not entirely deserved, nor erroneous, nor burdensome, the stigma nonetheless worked against the city's efforts to convince the rest of the nation that it was a decent place to live and a safe place to invest – that it was, in essence, just another good old American city.

Chief among the evidence to the contrary were antebellum pleasure spaces such as the infamous Gallatin Street and Sanctity Row near the French Market ["filled with low groggeries, the resort of the worst and most abandoned of both sexes"[1]], and 'The Swamp' and flatboat wharf on the sketchy fringes of uptown ["huckster shops, pigpens [and] gambling-shops"[2]]. French social geographer Elisée Réclus estimated "more than twenty-five hundred taverns" in New Orleans during his 1853 visit, and found them "always filled with drinkers...especially during election time."[3]

In postbellum times, New Orleans' brand of sensuality found an address on streets such as Basin and Franklin, which one source described as "slums and dives [with] the most loathsome, filthy, hotbeds of vice and debauchery ever permitted to befoul...any city," hosting "orgies...throughout the livelong night."[4] By 1897, pleasure had so broadly diffused that the city adopted a spatial solution to the sex trade as well as concert saloons [rollicking venues for music, dance, and drink] by legally limiting them to around the Basin and Franklin area. There, for the next 20 years, the nation's only legal red-light district, dubbed Storyville in sardonic honor of the alderman Sidney Story who came up with the idea, cinched New Orleans' reputation for decadence.

By the 1920s, however, as leisure tourism grew into an important economic sector, that nasty old repute, viewed through the sepia lens of romanticism and nostalgia, started to look less red and more green. What drew social condemnation in the 1800s now, in the 1900s, converted into valuable fiscal currency. The myth of carefree living, for example, became marketable as "The City That Care Forgot." Mardi Gras revelry became sellable as "America's Winter Wonderland." Musicality became profitable as "the birthplace of jazz," and local cooking customs found their way into pricey restaurants and became entertainment. Entrepreneurs in what we now call the hospitality industry joined forces with history lovers and municipal authorities to make space for this selectively remembered past. What resulted was a planned, zoned, and officially administered landscape of pleasure, with the architecturally protected French Quarter (Vieux Carre) and bawdy Bourbon Street gaining nationwide notoriety from the 1920s to 1940s. Even as the city as a whole benefitted from the economics behind the pleasure, many citizens were incensed by the vulgarity. "Look what they've done to one of the Vieux Carre's quiet thoroughfares!" beseeched a 1948 article titled "What's Happened to Bourbon Street?" "Bourbon's a bedlam...It's dirty, noisy and lusty...Every day and night there's a Mardi Gras going on somewhere along Bourbon street...If New Orleans is [the] 'city care forgot,' then this is [the] street where much forgetting took place!"[5]

By the 1970s to 2000s, pleasure spaces had expanded–courtesy historic renovation and gentrification, major events such as the 1984 Louisiana World Exposition, and the ever-growing tourism industry–such that by the new millennium, significant portions of the downtown cityscape were devoted to some form or another of the business of pleasure. In 2004, for the first time, visitation to New Orleans topped 10 million people, most of whom came seeking indulgence, even those ostensibly on business.

The flood following Hurricane Katrina in 2005 brought into relief just how intrinsic all this historical and contemporary pleasure mythology had become to the ethos of the city.[6] Nearly every mournful homage paid to the wrecked metropolis in the weeks after the deluge made some sort of reference to the city's *joie de vivre* (that French loanword making it all the more felicitous), and many subsequent arguments for rebuilding the city rested upon it (read Tom Piazza's *Why New Orleans Matters*). So fundamental had pleasure become to the city's culture and economy that, even as floodwaters remained in some neighborhoods, Mayor C. Ray Nagin proposed making more space for pleasure by inviting Vegas-style casinos into the urban core – on the highest and least-damaged terrain, no less. That idea got shot down, but the thinking behind it–of leveraging New Orleans' legacy of civic pleasure into cultural resilience and commercial opportunity–informed and illustrated the recovery. Find any post-Katrina planning document or

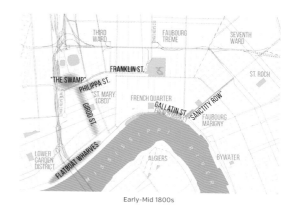

Early-Mid 1800s

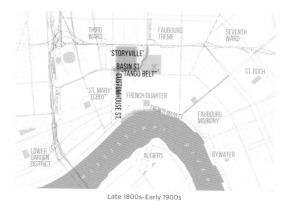

Late 1800s-Early 1900s

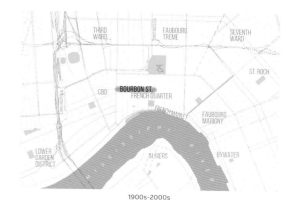

1900s-2000s

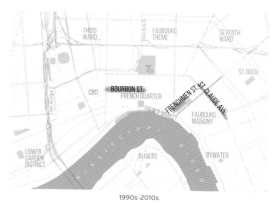

1990s-2010s

website of 2005–2006 vintage and you'll see profuse stock imagery of parading, drinking, eating, music-making, and dancing.

The recovery got off to a rough start, but eventually dollars started to arrive, opportunities started to open, and things began to change. A few thousand young planners, architects, urbanists, environmentalists, and social workers took leave from their graduate studies and nascent careers and headed south to be a part of something big, something important. Many took positions in the recovery efforts, or an alphabet soup of new nonprofits; some parlayed their experiences into Master's theses or PhD dissertations. This cohort largely moved on around 2008–2009, as recovery monies petered out and "new" became "new normal."[7]

By that time, however, a second wave began arriving. Enticed by the relatively robust regional economy compared to the rest of the recession-reeling nation, these newcomers were greater in number than the first wave, more specially skilled, and serious about planting roots here. They included a fair number of artists, musicians, chefs, and creative types who had turned their backs on homogenized mainstream America and resettled, like expatriates, in what they perceived to be an undiscovered bohemia somewhere south of the South and north of the Caribbean. Playing a key role in that perception was the city's legacy of exoticism and pleasure – the common denominator unifying everything from festivals, Carnival, and second-lines to bars, restaurants, and music venues.

Upon settling into local society, this vivacious lot, enamored by the city's mystique and self-selected for traits of Epicureanism and hedonism, returned the favor by, rather inevitably, creating their own pleasure spaces. What has resulted in the past few years is an ever-expanding landscape of hip live-music venues, trendy new eateries, coffee shops and bars, pop-ups, guerrilla performance venues, art spaces, gourmet food trucks, and street festivals (sanctioned or otherwise) appearing in neighborhoods that previously were the hard-scrapple domain of working-class families with neither the disposable income, nor the time, nor the cultural compatibility for such niceties. The most notable example, Bywater, has been described as "the Williamsburg of the South," and its adjacent artery of St. Claude has been called "the hippest avenue in America, according to *The New York Times*...hipsters with their tattoos and skinny jeans are everywhere..."[8] Restaurants with names like Sui Generis and bars such as Siberia have imported external foodie and indie-music influences, while "a group of bohemian artists [created] 'The Music Box: A Shantytown Sound Laboratory'" and kindred spirits have sprinkled the lower faubourgs with stuff like "The Tree House," a "healing center," yoga studios galore, "The Art House," and "a proposed Marigny ball pit house" derided as "a hipster Romper Room."[9]

Such are the newest features on New Orleans' 21st-century pleasure map. To be sure, few derive from local culture and many natives scorn them as the grating intrusions of outspoken outsiders from the rest of America. But then again, that's the sort of thing locals said about incoming Americans 200 years ago, after the Louisiana Purchase. That's the sort of thing disapproving traveloguists said about Gallatin Street, Sanctity Row, and the flatboat wharf 150 years ago. And that's what many New Orleanians said about Basin Street, Storyville, and Bourbon Street in the past 100 years. What we have today is in fact the latest cartography in New Orleans' 300-year-old atlas of pleasure.

1 Judith Kelleher Schafer, *Brothels, Depravity, and Abandoned Women: Illegal Sex in Antebellum New Orleans* [Baton Rouge: Louisiana State University Press, 2009], 6.

2 Journal of Welcome A. Greene, reproduced in "Being the Journal of a Quaker Merchant Who Visited N.O. in 1823," *Times-Picayune* [October 16, 1921], 6; James Stuart, *Three Years in North America*, Vol. II [1833], 232.

3 Elisée Réclus, *A Voyage to New Orleans*, eds. John Clark & Camille Martin [Thetford, Vermont, 2004 translation of 1855 original], 56–57.

4 "Some Sights in New Orleans the Harpers Didn't See," *The Mascot* [January 22, 1887], 2.

5 Ray Samuel, "What's Happened to Bourbon Street?," *Times-Picayune Magazine* [November 28, 1948], 8–11.

6 I use 'myth' here not to mean a falsehood, but rather a construct or perception that becomes 'real' over time through professional marketing, endless repetition, and sheer appeal.

7 I borrow here from my earlier article "Gentrification and Its Discontents: Notes from New Orleans," *New Geography* [March 1, 2013], http://www.newgeography.com/content/003526-gentrification-and-its-discontents-notes-new-orleans.

8 Susan Olasky, "New Orleans' New Identity, Nine Years After Katrina," *World* [August 29, 2014], http://www.worldmag.com/2014/08/new_orleans_new_identity_nine_years_after_katrina.

9 Doug MacCash, "A Bywater Lot Becomes 'The Music Box,' A Bohemian Musical Playground," *nola.com/The Times-Picayune* [October 20, 2011], http://www.nola.com/arts/index.ssf/2011/10/a_piety_street_lot_becomes_the.html; Kevin Allman, "More on the Marigny Ball Pit House," *Gambit* [April 25, 2012], http://www.bestofneworleans.com/blogofneworleans/archives/2012/04/25/more-on-the-marigny-ball-pit-house.

PLEASURE SPACE

Delivery of satellites into orbit was the primary driver of private space activity before the Ansari XPRIZE offered $10 million to any company that could launch a reusable vehicle into orbit twice in two weeks. The 2004 prize went to Mojave Aerospace Ventures SpaceShipOne, which has since been bought by Richard Branson as the new Virgin Galactic flagship.

The commercial space industry is in its infancy but early investment in tourism is a positive indicator. A new spaceport built by architecture firm Foster and Partners has appeared in the New Mexico desert, while a Dutch entrepreneur plans to send contestants on a one-way trip to Mars for a reality television show. Despite this surge in activity, the risks of space flight are still real. A fatal Virgin Galactic test flight in October 2014 has raised new doubts about the company's future.

The pleasure tourism horizon is expanding and for a few hundred thousand dollars, you too can see the curvature of the earth.

BIGELOW AEROSPACE
ORBITAL, 10 – 60 DAYS
$26.25 – $36.75 MILLION

KARMAN LINE = 62MI

VIRGIN GALACTIC
SUB-ORBITAL, 6 MINUTES
$250,000

XCOR SPACE
SUB-ORBITAL
$95,000

Space Port America

Mojave Air & Space Port

Sources: ansari.xprize.org; spaceportamerica.com; www.mars-one.com; www.space.com; www.bigelowaerospace.com; xcor.com; an

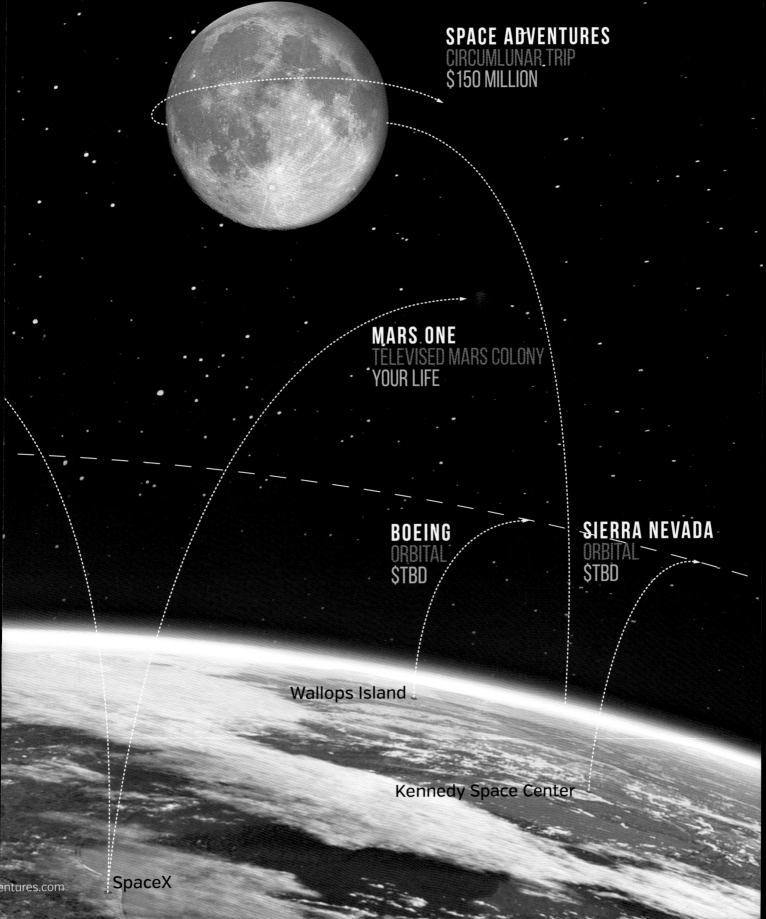

SPACE ADVENTURES
CIRCUMLUNAR TRIP
$150 MILLION

MARS ONE
TELEVISED MARS COLONY
YOUR LIFE

BOEING
ORBITAL
$TBD

SIERRA NEVADA
ORBITAL
$TBD

Wallops Island

Kennedy Space Center

SpaceX

IMAGE CREDITS

Endpapers

"The Triumph of Pan" (1636) by Nicolas Poussin, © The National Gallery, London/Art Resource, used with permission.

Editorial

p. 4: "New Babylon – Den Haag" (1964) by Constant Nieuwenhuys, from the Gemeentemuseum Collection, used with permission.

What is Pleasure?

p. 7: "The Fall of Man" (1570) by Titian (public domain).
p. 9: "Core" by (and courtesy of) Chieh Huang.

An Architecture of Pleasure and Pain

p. 10–11: "From Within" (2006) by Annie Cattrell, used with permission.
p. 13, 16: "Pleasure/Pain" (2010) by Annie Cattrell (in collaboration with Morten Kringelbach), used with permission.
p. 14: Figures of MRI mapping of pleasure and pain in the brain courtesy Morten Kringelbach.
p. 15: "Sense" (2002–2004) by Annie Cattrell (in collaboration with Morten Kringelbach, Mark Lythgoe, and Steve Smith), used with permission.

Bread and Circuses

p. 18–19: "Church at the Baths of Diocletian" by Aaron Kimberlin, used with permission.
p. 22–23: "Map of Campus Martius" by Robert Adam (public domain).
p. 25: "Columns of St Peters" by Aaron Kimberlin, used with permission.
p. 26: "The Bathing Pool" by Hubert Robert, The Metropolitan Museum of Art, Gift of J. Pierpont Morgan, 1917 (www.metmuseum.org).

Urban Pleasures

p. 28–29: "Across" by (and courtesy of) Chieh Huang.
p. 30, 32: Images of the Situationist Drawing Device by Ji Soo Han and Paul Ornsby, used with permission.

Notes on a City Built for Pleasure

p. 34–35: "Aero View of Atlantic City, New Jersey" (1909) by Hughes and Bailey (public domain).

Dream City: London's Pleasurescapes

p. 38–39: Docklands collage by (and courtesy of) Cricket Day.
p. 41: Image of the Flip Flap (1908), courtesy Josephine Kane.
p. 44: Render of scheme for Battersea Power Station, London by Atelier Zündel Cristea, used with permission.

The Evolving Architecture of Pleasure

p. 46: "Vegas" by (and courtesy of) Cricket Day.
p. 48–51: Historic plans of the Strip by (and courtesy of) Cricket Day; icons © Stefan Al, courtesy of Stefan Al.

In Conversation with Jerry Van Eyck

p. 54–59: Images © !melk Landscape Architecture, courtesy !melk Landscape Architecture.

Pleasure Pit

p. 62: Image of diamond ring © Michael Christensen, used with permission.

Spatial Regulation of the Sex Industry in NYC

p. 64–65: "New York Dolls" by Leanne Staples, www.leannestaples.com, used with permission.
p. 66–67: Composite by Richard Fisher using images "Manhattan Barcode" by DZZN and "Trish0050" by Marco Leone, used under CC BY-NC-SA 2.0 license via flickr.com.
p. 68: Mapping of New York City Sex Industry by (and courtesy of) Richard Fisher.
p. 70: "Midtown Manhattan" (1973) by Chester Higgins, US National Archives (public domain).

Pleasure Craft

p. 73: "Sonnenanbeter" by Olivier Rüegsegger, www.rieggi.ch, used with permission.
p. 75: "Aerial of Brooklyn Bridge Park, New York" by Alex S. MacLean (2010), used with permission.
p. 77: "Hammock Grove, Governors Island, New York" by Timothy Schenck, used with permission (original image desaturated).
p. 78: "Aerial view of High Line from West 30th Street" by Iwan Baan (2011), courtesy Friends of the High Line/James Corner Field Operations.
p. 79: "Sitting on the High Line" (2011) by Matthew Pillsbury, used with permission. Courtesy Matthew Pillsbury and Benrubi Gallery, New York.
p. 81: Map of projects by (and courtesy of) Cricket Day.

Why so Serious, Landscape Architect?

p. 83: Excerpt from "After A Sunday Service in St. Louis" by Charles Upham, © Bettmann/CORBIS, used with permission.

Shaping, Experiencing, and Escaping the Tourist City

p. 86–87: Collage of vintage tourist posters (public domain) by Richard Fisher.

State of the World

p. 90: Catalogue of islands of "The World," Dubai, by (and courtesy of) Cricket Day.

p. 91: "Artificial Archipelagos, Dubai, United Arab Emirates" by NASA Johnson Space Center (public domain).

The Pleasure Drive

p. 92: "Lookout Mountain Drive, Denver," Denver Mountain Parks Brochure (1916), courtesy Denver Mountain Parks Collection and Paul Daniel Marriott.

p. 94: "Henry Hudson Parkway, New York," Gilmore Clarke Papers (1947), courtesy Columbia University and Paul Daniel Marriott.

Resort Urbanism

p. 96–101: Images of Discovery Bay by (and courtesy of) Scott Jennings Melbourne.

p. 100: Master plan of Discovery Bay, courtesy HKRI Ltd. and Scott Jennings Melbourne.

The Edge of Pleasure

p. 102: "Pool with a View" by Joseph Younis (2010), www.josephyounis.com, used under CC BY-NC-SA 2.0 license via flickr.com.

p. 103: "Site Plan of Marina Bay" by Lucas Butcher (2014), courtesy Adrianne Joergensen.

p. 104–105: "Marina Bay Sands: Lights and Lasers" by Joseph Dsilva (2012), used under CC BY-NC-SA 2.0 license via flickr.com.

Prora

p. 106: Image of Prora by Stefan Andreas, used with permission.

The Air We Breathe

p. 108–109: Photograph of MONA by Leigh Carmichael, courtesy Museum of Old and New Art, Tasmania, Australia.

p. 110: "The Void" by Matt Newton, courtesy Museum of Old and New Art, Tasmania, Australia.

p. 112–113: Photograph of Nolan Gallery and "Snake" (artist: Sidney Nolan, Australia, 1970–1972) by Rémi Chauvin, courtesy Museum of Old and New Art, Tasmania, Australia.

p. 114–115: Photograph of "Cloaca Professional" (artist: Wim Delvoye, Belgium, 2010) by Rémi Chauvin, courtesy Museum of Old and New Art, Tasmania, Australia.

Playground for a Drug Lord

p. 116: Playground render by (and courtesy of) Richard Fisher.

p. 117: Aerial view of Hacienda Nápoles © Google. Map data © CNES/Astrium, 2014.

p. 117: "Entrada a la Hacienda Napoles" by XaID, used under CC BY 3.0 license via wikicommons; "Hippopotami" by FICG.mx, used under CC BY 2.0 license via flickr.com; "Dinosaurs," "Hacienda Napoles," and "Africa Museum" by Paula Funnell, used under CC BY 2.0 license via flickr.com; "Hacienda Napoles" by la mujer elefante, used under CC BY-NC-SA 2.0 license via flickr.com.

Pleasure Crops

p. 118–119: Pleasure crops mapping by (and courtesy of) Chieh Huang.

In Conversation with Vladimir Sitta

p. 120–125: Images courtesy Vladimir Sitta/Terragram.

Pleasure Atlas

p. 126–127: "New Orleans By Night" by (and courtesy of) Richard Fisher.

p. 128: Maps by (and courtesy of) Richard Fisher and Richard Campanella.

Pleasure Space

p. 130: "Pleasure Space" by (and courtesy of) Cricket Day.

p. 134: "Map of Science derived from Clickstream Data" by Bollen J, Van de Sompel H, Hagberg A, Bettencourt L, Chute R, et al. (2009) "Clickstream Data Yields High-Resolution Maps of Science", *PLoS ONE* 4(3): e4803. doi: 10.1371/journal.pone.0004803, used under CC BY license.

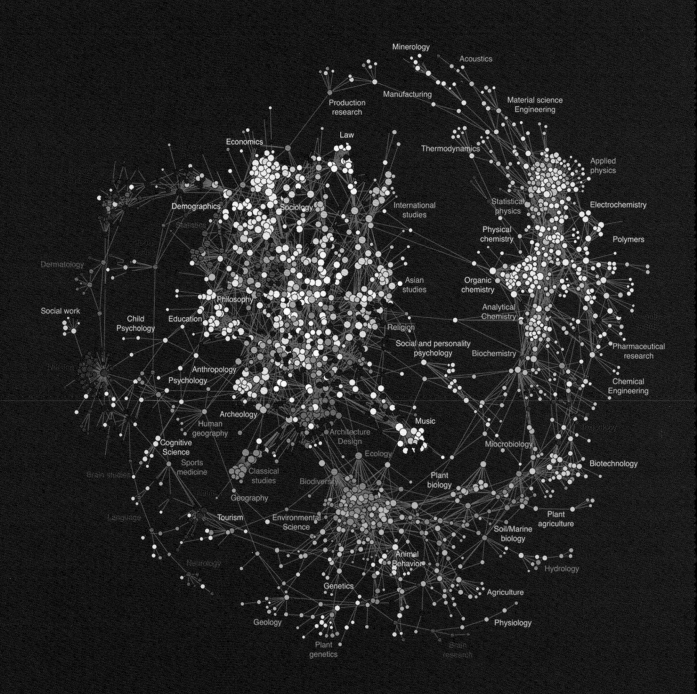

WILD SPRING 2015

PLEASURE FALL 2015

TYRANNY SPRING 2016

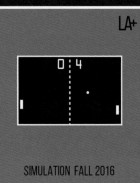

SIMULATION FALL 2016

INTERDISCIPLINARY JOURNAL
OF LANDSCAPE ARCHITECTURE

IDENTITY SPRING 2017

UPCOMING ISSUES

LA+ (Landscape Architecture Plus) from the University of Pennsylvania School of Design is the first truly interdisciplinary journal of landscape architecture. Within its pages you will hear not only from designers, but also from historians, artists, philosophers, psychologists, geographers, sociologists, planners, scientists, and others. Our aim is to reveal connections and build collaborations between landscape architecture and other disciplines by exploring each issue's theme from multiple perspectives.

LA+ brings you a rich collection of contemporary thinkers and designers in two issues each year. To subscribe follow the links at WWW.LAPLUSJOURNAL.COM